I # NAKED

II # IN

III # GOD'S

IV # HOLY

V # TEMPLE

Exposing your deepest insecurities to reach your truest potential

————————— BY MATT ZIELICH

For Kieren & Kinsley

May you take into consideration the full life that comes from wholeheartedly following Jesus in a world that makes convincing promises by offering synthetic alternatives.

The choice is yours to make.

CONTENTS

INTRODUCTION

He Came at Night

No one would refute the historical impact of Jesus of Nazareth. The fact that we still mention his name today is impressive, to say the least. How was a humble man, from an insignificant region, without notable status, able to leave such a massive imprint on civilization?

There are many answers to that question, but regardless of what you believe about him, it is clear that he left an impression on the people he encountered.

He challenged them to expand their perspective. He confronted the powers of oppression. He diagnosed the root cause of significant problems. He critiqued the beliefs and systems that enabled corruption. He worked to define and restore the dignity of all people.

As the ministry of Jesus traveled throughout the area, the crowds grew to witness him firsthand. As you could imagine, there was a fair amount of skepticism when rumors of miracles and healings were spreading. Some gathered for hope, some for intrigue, some for doubt, and some for …

Fear.

Some were afraid it was only rumors. That their hope would diminish. That this man from Nazareth would be just like so many others—to come and not deliver on their promises. That excitement would quickly fade back into the normalcy of life. That the problems faced would not be conquered and the challenges of today would perpetuate to tomorrow.

Some were afraid it wasn't true.

But some were afraid that it *was*.

Why would anyone fear the arrival of the promised messiah? Isn't this good news?

Well, not for everyone.

Some people caught a good enough glimpse of Jesus to fear the kingdom that he wanted to build. To fear his disregard of man-made tradition. To fear his confrontation of the injustice that granted some people power. To fear the way he challenged the authority of those with high positions.

People like the Pharisees.

It's clear that many of these religious leaders feared Jesus to the point of conspiring to get him killed. The prospect of Jesus as messiah threatened to take everything they had built. And when another kingdom threatens to invade, it becomes a violent battle.

But not all the Pharisees were against Jesus. Some witnessed his miracles and listened to his teachings and wanted to explore the possibility that he was who he said he was—the Son of God, savior of the world.

That's what we find in a story in John 3. Here, we are introduced to a Pharisee named Nicodemus who was curious about Jesus, so he went to visit with him …

At night.

This might be a small detail, but it says a lot. Why would Nicodemus wait until sundown to speak to Jesus?

So he wouldn't be seen.

As a religious leader, he felt the pressure to protect his position. What would people think if they saw him with Jesus? Why would people seek his guidance once they realized he sought guidance himself? The burden of perception is heavy and many work hard to hide their legs shaking under the weight.

Nighttime is when you won't be seen. When you can hide. When you won't be exposed.

And what's at the heart of these intentions?

Insecurity.

Nicodemus was insecure that the people who knew and respected him would think less of him if they witnessed him learning from Jesus.

But it's hard to blame Nicodemus. Can't we cut him some slack? He lived in a world where he was under the microscope. Back then, people had to protect their reputation. They had to grow their following. They had to expand their influence. They had to manage their image. They had to accomplish great things. They had to fight to be noticed.

It was nothing like today …

Thank God we don't live in a world where we feel the pressure to keep up appearances. Aren't you glad you can make choices without worrying about what people will think of you? Aren't you grateful you don't ever feel the need to chase validation through accomplishments or approval? Isn't it great we have dismantled social hierarchy and enabled all people to feel secure in their own identities?

Are you picking up on the sarcasm here?

Truthfully, I still find myself tip-toeing toward Jesus the same way as Nicodemus—at night. It's my way of having a foot in two kingdoms. I want to protect my position, influence, plans, and agenda while being close to Jesus. But this approach doesn't really work. That's why Jesus told Nicodemus one of the scariest things he's ever said in his entire ministry. He tells Nicodemus that he needs to be …

Born again.[1]

Well sure, if you're thinking like Nicodemus, who wouldn't be afraid of the prospect of squeezing back into the womb? But this instruction actually becomes a bit *more* terrifying once you find out Jesus wasn't speaking literally.

If the idea of being born again—even metaphorically—doesn't scare you, then I wonder if you truly understand the implications of what Jesus was saying. Let me explain.

When my son was born, I remember staring at him in the crib next to my sleeping wife in the hospital. His eyes were open. Like, wide open. He didn't really sleep for the first few hours after delivery. He just quietly stared, adapting to his new senses that were finally working cohesively to form an awareness of himself and his surroundings.

The whole time I watched him, I couldn't help but wonder … *What is he thinking?*

And then it occurred to me there was literally no way I could possibly imagine. Here's why.

Everything I thought my son might be thinking came from a mind that was already acquainted with its environment. I had a vocabulary and the ability to reconcile with my surroundings.

On the contrary, my son didn't even know *who* he was. Honestly, he didn't even know *that* he was.

He had no established framework. Everything—even down to his own senses—was new.

He didn't know the sounds around him. He didn't know the face staring back at him. He didn't know he was a son. All these things had to be taught. He would have to slowly awaken to the reality of his own existence.

Whatever I imagined he was thinking, I was assuredly wrong. My knowledge and self-awareness had inhibited my ability to process a genuinely fresh view of the world.

That's what Jesus is really saying to Nicodemus. To be born again is to see the world with fresh eyes. To listen with fresh ears. And in order to make this possible, it means he'd have to unlearn what he already knew. He would have to deconstruct his understanding of the world and of himself.

That's a terrifying instruction. It means stripping away all the information and perspectives we've accumulated over the years. It means relinquishing the worldview we've adopted that's helped us reconcile to our existence. It means letting go of a way of thinking that we've established to protect ourselves all our life. And to do so would certainly make us feel …

Naked.

Jesus commends Nicodemus and respects his position, but there was something in the way of him reaching his full potential. Nicodemus thought that there was some kind of new or hidden knowledge that he needed to acquire from Jesus. But the solution wasn't addition—it was subtraction. He needed to unlearn what he knew. He needed a brand new perspective. He needed fresh eyes. He needed to start over. He needed to be …

Born again.

"Born again Christian" sounds like something you'd hear from a sweaty southern preacher that you fear cares more about your money than your eternal soul. And if that's the picture your mind generates, then you'll have to unlearn that, as well. Because these words first belonged to Jesus, and he wasn't trying to get your wallet; he was trying to align you with the way—his way.

We need to become helpless infants, minutes fresh into a new world. We need to strip away the layers that inhibit our senses. We need new eyes, new ears, a new mind, and a new heart.

We need to be told who we are by our father. We may not see him clearly because our eyes haven't quite formed, but we can recognize his voice. It's the one that's been speaking over us from the beginning while we awaited departure from the womb.

Maybe you feel a bit like Nicodemus—cautiously optimistic. Maybe you find yourself lending Jesus your intrigue, respect, or adoration, yet you are too fearful or insecure to approach in the daylight. Truthfully, we all approach Jesus under the cover of NIGHT:

Naked
In
God's
Holy
Temple.

This is our framework to start over—the pathway to the life Jesus is offering. To move past our insecurities. To receive a vision of hope. To see God in new ways. To encounter truth. To reach our full potential.

So let's begin.

But first, you'll need to get …

PART I

NAKED

|nā-kəd| |nakid|
Adjective

1 (Of a person or part of the body) without clothes.
(Of an object) without the usual covering or protection.
(Of a tree, plant, or animal) without leaves, hairs, scales, shell, etc.
Exposed to harm, unprotected, or vulnerable.

2 (Of something such as feelings or behavior) undisguised, blatant.

Don't Look at My Private Parts

I was a late bloomer. This meant that all through middle school, while guys around me were growing armpit hair and forming muscle definition, I remained hairless and had a body like a noodle. Some of the guys started growing patchy beards and looked like they were heading out for an *MTV Spring Break* party. I looked like I was venturing out for a delightful afternoon to Chuck E. Cheese and then maybe a nap after all the excitement.

I'm not sure if you remember puberty, but it's an incredibly awkward time for all of us. Your body is changing. Your hormones are raging. And all this is happening inside an organism still trying to find its place and rank among the others.

I had an extremely high awareness of the pace guys and girls were developing around me, and I felt like I was way back in last place. Because of this, there was one dreaded room more terrifying than all the rest:

The locker room.

Back when you were in elementary school, P.E. was one of the best classes of the day. It functioned as an additional recess. When the bell rang, you would run straight to the gymnasium and await instructions—praying it was the day they broke out that massive multicolored parachute blanket you would run underneath before it collapsed to the ground.[1] But by the time you graduated into middle school, a new step was added to the process.

In middle school, before you could throw a ball or climb a rope you had to remove your shirt, drop your pants, and change into gym clothes.

If that never bothered you, congratulations. You probably had abs and already started kissing with tongue. But for the rest of us, we remember shielding our bodies in the corner and trying not to get caught sneaking a peek at everyone else for comparison.

You could take the easy route and be the kid that gathered their clothes and sprinted into the bathroom stall, but I always found that drew more attention to yourself, not less. My method was to find the most remote section of the locker room, turn my body away from everyone around me, and swap my wardrobe like I was putting out a fire. I was a NASCAR pit-crew member changing the tires on a first-place Gen-6 with only a few laps to go.

Two-point-three seconds. Clothed.

But after eighth grade, it got worse—*communal showers.*

Around this time I became a very spiritual person with a vibrant prayer life. My conversations with the Lord sounded something like this: "Please God, kill me."

The last method of hiding would be to wear your bathing suit in the shower, but this strategy came at a great cost. Let's just say it would not bode well for your social ranking.

As a 14-year-old freshman, this paralyzed me. Now everyone was going to see my, you know …

P-E-E P-E-E.

I couldn't bear it. Insecurity was an understatement. I decided that I would skip the showers and stink for the rest of the day. Control what you can and accept the consequence. It was certainly preferable to the possibility of being the target of everyone's penis jokes.

At that age, it was an absolute nightmare to stand naked before others. But then again, not much has changed into adulthood. Sure, your body matures, and you no longer feel nervous stepping into a locker room—but exposing skin and private parts isn't the only way to feel naked.

There are parts of you that you've spent your whole life covering up. They are protected behind an impenetrable fortress you've built— designed to hide the insecurities you won't let anyone see. These are some of your thoughts, desires, ideas, dreams, or past mistakes. We lock them away and hide the key. They possess confidential information that outlines some of the deepest—and if we're honest—*most authentic* parts of who we are.

Imagine walking around tomorrow with a display over your head that broadcasts every thought you've ever had for all to see. Or maybe your online search history? Or your sexual fantasies? Or your private conversations? Or your opinions of different ethnic groups? Or the dreams you have never shared with anyone? Or the people you love? Or the people you hate?

Those are things that you can't allow to get out. It could ruin you. It would make you vulnerable, and vulnerability feels a lot like weakness. Best to cover it up, right?

We all keep a diary. An outline of our authentic selves inked out in our unique handwriting. Some of us write it in a journal but the rest write it in our minds. A diary in the wrong hands would be very destructive. Who can you trust? If you listen to your insecurities, you'll get a clear answer: no one but yourself.

Our society seems to celebrate the notion of authenticity, but it's all a mirage. A tricky image we cling to in the desert. Who wants to go out on a limb and risk it snapping under the weight of the truth?

So we all just smile and pretend we're acting authentically because no one knows we're fake. No one knows we aren't worthy—that we don't belong.

And if no one knows we don't belong, then we can maintain the facade that we do.

Could you imagine if everyone said what they were thinking? Despite how good of a person you think you are, just audit the mental toxicity that fills your mind when you're trying to get ahold of your cable provider—the one that overcharged you *again*—and they're dodging your confrontation through circuits of automated instructions that offer no options to speak to a real person.[2]

Situations like that bring out the worst in all of us.

Can you imagine telling everyone how you *really* felt? Those conversations would leave a trail of broken relationships as long as the span of your life. So you learn at a young age to filter what you say. You take a moment to evaluate your thoughts and determine which ones would be received well and which ones would leave you feeling exposed.

We are all very complicated humans. What we allow others to see is only a fraction of what's going on under the surface. The things we think, consider, process, and explore, without anyone knowing, make up a large percentage of who we are.

Don't get me wrong, some of that *should* be protected. I'm not saying you should go out to the world and expose yourself. Don't do that figuratively, and especially don't do that literally.

The point I'm trying to make is this: at some level, we all have insecurities we're trying to hide. We all have vulnerabilities we're trying to protect. We all have pain and guilt and shame we're trying to bury.

No matter how old we are or how much we've accomplished, we all find ourselves in moments looking over our shoulder, hoping no one sees us …

Naked.

A Brief History of Nudity

You were born naked.

That means you were seen naked. And not just by your parents. In the first few years of your life, there were probably several people who saw you naked. Doctors, grandparents, cousins, siblings. None of this even phased you.

At a young age, humans haven't even developed a sense of awareness. Bath time? Make it a party. Need to go potty? Hose down the grass. Have to change at the beach? Drop your pants in the open air.

For the first few years of your life, you can be naked just about anywhere. In those years, it's cute, and no one minds.

But then at some point, things progressively change.

You aren't allowed to run around naked anymore. You can't share baths. You can't change your clothes openly on the beach. There isn't quite a definitive age, and the tendencies vary between different cultures, but somewhere in your childhood, you began to feel the need to cover up. You couldn't let people see you naked.

Why is that? Two obvious reasons.

Sex and intimacy.

Let's focus on sex first because that one is easier. The Bible says that God created you as a human to have sexual desire. His very first instruction to human beings was to make a baby. Make lots of babies.[3] Through the method of ...

Sex.

Wow. The Bible starts on a pretty good note. And this is a natural part of your physical, mental, and emotional development. Arousal of this desire is through the means of attraction. Many things determine the attraction, but perhaps none more than sight.[4] When you see someone that you consider attractive, you become aroused, which triggers your sexual desire. This process is simple human biology. If this is news to you, then allow me to present my most persuasive argument against homeschooling.[5]

Think back to any moment of your life when you became so completely transfixed on someone that you couldn't take your eyes off of them. Maybe you stole glances when they walked past you at the store or the gym or the pool. The temptation to stare exists for a reason. There is something about them physically that is alerting you to track them.

And that's with clothes *on.* Can you imagine if they were naked?

Of course you could!

That's the point. Your sight would instantaneously alert your arousal, and you'd notice your sexual desire skyrocket. That's one easy answer to why you can't walk around naked. That level of visual stimulation wouldn't be healthy for our society.[6]

But if you keep reading, you'll see that sex isn't even the most significant reason that we can't walk around naked. Genesis tells a story of God's design for marriage through the couple Adam and Eve. As their bond of marriage is sealed in their physical union, it says that they were naked but felt no shame.[7]

So what changed?

Genesis tells the story like this:

God placed Adam and Eve in a garden and gave them the responsibility to watch over it. To cultivate the land and govern the animals. There was a plentiful supply of food from the trees, but God created a boundary. There was only one tree they were instructed not to eat from: the tree of knowledge of good and evil.

But then something new enters the story.

Doubt.

It comes in the voice of a serpent that entices Adam and Eve to challenge God's boundary.

They eat the forbidden fruit, and it opens their eyes.

Before this moment, they were naked and felt no shame. Then, Adam and Eve suddenly felt exposed and insecure. They tried to cover themselves with fig leaves and hid in the bushes.

This story has been passed down throughout the generations because it identifies a universal problem:

Intimacy.

This reason is much more complicated because it reaches to the level of *identity*—the foundations of who you are. It's the closeness of knowing and being known.

If you take a secular worldview, you might feel that you are nothing more than a body—a collection of cells formed by atoms occupied in space and time.

But if you believe that there is more to you than simple matter—that there is a *spirit* in your being—then your body is only one layer of who you are. There is a part of you that isn't flesh and bone. A part that began in the mind of God from the moment he thought you should exist. This part of you won't wither or die. This part of you is eternal.

There is something extraordinarily intimate about standing naked in front of someone. You're uncovered. Fully exposed. You are fully seen and more than in an exclusively physical sense.

Being naked is more than just revealing your body. It's revealing your innermost soul.

Intimacy demands to be honored. But what if it isn't? What if you expose yourself and end up hurt? It's too risky.

So you decide to be guarded. In a world now full of shame, you feel the instinct to conceal your whole, authentic self. You hide your intimate thoughts. You find a way to mask them. You find a place to hide.

You were born naked and unaware. But things have changed. Now you know. Now you have eyes to see.

It's time to cover up.

Why Is the Statue of David Naked?

Resting inside the Galleria dell'Accademia di Firenze is Michelangelo's statue of *David*.

This impressive marble sculpture is notable for a variety of reasons. The sculpture was originally commissioned to sit atop the Florence Cathedral. It was created with significant detail, but because of complications, ended up next to the Palazzo Vecchio entrance.

When you see the statue, you might notice a few important details. The head and hands are disproportionately more massive than the body. The figure carries a sling and looks outward with a somber expression. The veins in his arms bulge, and his posture indicates a feeling of tension.

Oh yeah. And he's...

Naked.

What makes this work of art unique among other depictions of the biblical David is that it portrays the character *before* his battle with Goliath. While other works often capture the moments of his famous victory, this one is powerful because it reveals the hero's resolve in the face of a terrifying foe with an uncertain outcome.

The story of David and Goliath is familiar. The quick summary is that David—a young shepherd boy—against unlikely odds slays Goliath, the Philistine giant. Whenever we talk about David and Goliath, it's usually to inspire hope for the underdog against impossible odds.

But there is a much more substantial layer of this story than the outcome of the battle. Let's turn to 1 Samuel 17. When King Saul's army is suited for combat, Goliath mocks them. He towers over nine feet tall and wears armor weighing well over a hundred pounds. He marches out ahead of his army, seeking a challenger, but no one dares to step forward. Until the young boy David, a lowly shepherd and the youngest of eight, was willing to accept the challenge.

The texts says, "Then [king] Saul gave David his armor—a bronze helmet and a coat of mail. David put it on, strapped the sword over it, and took a step or two to see what it was like, for he had never worn such things before."[8]

David is wrapped up in armor for a purpose, and that purpose is *protection.*

It is intended to keep him safe from the weapons of his enemy.

That's why armor was invented. To keep us safe against threats of harm.

We wear armor all the time, but not of steel and bronze. The armor we wear is metaphorical. We construct mental and emotional armor to protect us from feeling vulnerable to the things we perceive as threatening. We hide behind coverings of our own making because it provides us the feeling of safety from the mental and emotional dangers of our surroundings.
The giants we face might not be named Goliath, but they certainly are terrifying. And so it seems like a wise strategy to approach our giants behind the protection of bronze and steel.[9]

But that's not what David does.

"I can't fight in these," he protested to Saul. "I'm not used to them." So David took them off.

For David to win this battle, he decides **it's better to strip the armor off rather than strap it on.**

Beyond the distinct physical advantage (removing the armor allows him to move more quickly and freely to gain the upper hand in battle), there is also a spiritual layer that provides us with valuable insight.

When we strip our armor and stand naked before God, we are the strongest. Removing our coverings is *how* we receive the victory.

But we craft this armor because we think we can trust in it to protect us. If we remove our coverings, it means placing our trust in something else. Something other than our strength or in the power of the armor we create.

It means placing our trust in God.

And there is nothing harder than *trusting* when we feel exposed and unprotected.

But truthfully, that's the only time trust can exist. It's not real until we let our guard down and make ourselves vulnerable. Otherwise, we don't need faith. That's why we hide behind the walls we've put up.

Regardless of where we're at with God, we can all agree that a healthy and significant relationship with him cannot exist without trust. That's true of any relationship.

That's why I—and millions of others through history—find Michelangelo's depiction of David so inspiring. It's the balance of vulnerability and strength. Exposure and courage. Insecurity and confidence.

Naked—yet somehow—clothed.

It's the posture we need to take with God. To remove our armor and stand naked before him, revealing who we truly are. This is no easy task. This is the hardest part of following Jesus.

I think that's worth saying again:

Trusting God enough to let him see you naked, standing before him and fully exposing your thoughts, feelings, insecurities, mistakes, failures, regrets, dreams, visions, goals, desires—everything—is the hardest part of following Jesus.

It. Is. The. Hardest. Part.

Think about that. The Christian life isn't easy by any stretch of the imagination. But if this is true, then consider all the things that don't top the list.

Generosity. Spiritual disciplines. Sexual purity. Serving. Tithing. Forgiveness. Loving your enemies. Persecution. Selling all your possessions.

All of these are secondary to trusting God.

Don't get me wrong—the list of things we do when we follow Jesus are all things that are extremely difficult. The point isn't to claim they are easy.

The point is to realize that once you take the hardest step of trusting God—that he is good and his way is genuinely best—then all of the difficult things we do to obey Jesus are validated.

Of course, it's still challenging to forgive someone who has wronged you or to be generous to others. But if you *trust* God, then doing any of these things carries the assurance you're on a specific path that will take you where you truly want to go.

The gateway to life is very narrow, and the road is arduous—only a few ever find it.[10]

But when we trust in God the way David did—when we remove our armor and make ourselves vulnerable—we will have our most significant victory. We can then shed the unnecessary weight of our coverings and conquer our shame and insecurity.

But before we can have this victory, we need to find an answer to a fundamental question:

Who Told You That You Were Naked?

Curiosity is in our nature, and humans have always asked questions to understand our existence better. You probably have a list of questions you'd ask God if given a chance.

And you're not alone.

The world is full of books written about the questions people have for God. That comes as no surprise. But consider this:

The Bible is a library of books filled with questions God has for *us.*

Some of the questions God asks are subtle while others are direct. But these questions are crucial for our understanding of what it means to be human. Jesus often responded to a question with another question.

And there is a reason.

Questions are essential to our personal growth and development. Humans are particularly impressive among the created order if only for our ability to inquire about the world. Questions help us dig into the layers that lie beneath our knowledge. They function to sharpen our minds with wisdom and insight. Questions target our ignorance and help us expand our understanding. Curiosity is a primary tool that aims to help us navigate a path toward maturity. All humans ask questions to reconcile the nature of their existence with their individual experiences.

God asks questions. Not because *he* needs answers.

We do.

His inquiry is a strategy that he intends to leverage for our development. When God asks questions, it's for our benefit, not his. When we see a question in the Bible, we must pay attention because there is something important God wants us to discover.

In the Bible, the first two questions God asks humans are in Genesis. In the opening pages, we learn that God creates all things and makes humans in his image. He gives them order and boundaries along with the agency of free will. If you're familiar with the story, you'll remember that Adam and Eve cross the only boundary they are given. They taste the forbidden fruit from the tree of the knowledge of good and evil, and something happens.

They feel shame at their nakedness.

Notice that being naked wasn't the problem. They were naked all along. God created them this way. Free and confident to be exactly how he designed them. To stand uncovered and unguarded in his presence and the presence of one another. Before this moment, they were naked *but felt no shame.*[11]

This act of rebellion gave birth to something foreign to God's design for his people. Something was created in his world, but God didn't create it. Before Adam and Eve were obedient to God's command to create new human life, they created something else first:

Insecurity.

Insecurity didn't exist in the world God created. It was forged by the human will—to be like God and define good and evil for themselves.

So this is where God asks the first two questions in the Bible. Let's start with the second one first:

"Who told you that you were naked?"[12]

In other words, what is the source of your insecurity? Where did it originate? How did you come to feel this way?

In case it isn't clear—according to God—the source of human shame and insecurity is a *who*.

Before you start jumping to conclusions, let's remember to slow down. When God asks a question, it's not because he doesn't know the answer. It's because we don't. At least not yet. Questions help guide us towards growth and development.

So. Who is responsible?

According to Adam, it was his wife.[13] His instinct in a moment of vulnerability is to blame Eve and to pass responsibility. Isn't that what insecurity does? It makes us feel exposed, and our only means of protection is redirecting the blame elsewhere. It's the same thing Eve does. Her insecurity causes her to pass responsibility to the serpent.[14]

Maybe you struggle with the Bible because you're not into the whole "talking snake" thing. Those issues are important, but not more important than the message behind the story, and here it is:

There is a personal force with a plan in direct opposition to God's will for humans.[15]

Jesus names this force the Adversary. You might know it by the name Satan or the Devil. But here it's the serpent, and if you allow yourself to get too caught up in the logistics of this story's history, you'll miss the cautionary warning:

This force is coming after *you.*

At this point, you might think, *Of course! That's the answer to God's second question! It's the serpent that tells them they were naked. It was all his fault; what a mean little snake.*

We all better watch out for that manipulative voice but probably not in the way you'd expect because here's the twist:

It wasn't the serpent.

"At that moment, their eyes opened, *and they suddenly felt shame* at their nakedness. So they sewed fig leaves together to cover themselves."[16]

Who told them they were naked?

No one.

No pointing fingers. No sideways glances. No condemning remarks. Shame awoke in the silence of their developing self-awareness.

Our ambition to become like God makes us the architect of our insecurity.

The serpent has a different role and one that should elevate our caution. He doesn't bring direct opposition to God's warning. All he does is plant a seed of doubt to God's goodness with his question:

Did God really say …?[17]

Put another way—*do you agree his way is best? Could he be holding out? Can you trust him? What if a better life is available with a kingdom of your own making?*

The serpent doesn't need to tell you that you're naked. He says your God can't be trusted, and if you believe him, you'll decide you're naked all by yourself.

He doesn't give them a list of sins to commit. He doesn't tell them everything God doesn't want them to do. Instead, he convinces them to create a world where they make the rules.

Where they become a judge. Where they define morality. Where they establish what is right.

Make no mistake, the serpent is not innocent. God condemns his actions and sentences him to be crushed under the heel of Jesus.[18] But the serpent's guilt doesn't correlate with our innocence. We play a part in our destruction.

Creating Insecurity

Humans were not taught how to be sinful. They were simply invited to challenge the boundaries God set in place. And what is on the other side? The unclaimed territory where we can establish our kingdom.

The Bible calls this sin.

Maybe that sounds like a dirty word or a manipulative exaggeration designed to target your mistakes or flaws. But the term comes from the Greek word *hamartia*, "missing the mark" like when you're shooting at a target.

But every use of this term concerns ethics. When it comes to determining what is right and wrong, our sin is the result of missing the mark.

And what is this mark we're supposed to be targeting?

Human flourishing. The absolute best way for people to live and thrive.

That means sin isn't just doing bad things. Sin is the fundamental source of what is diminishing our quality of life and the lives of those around us. When we want to redefine good and evil or give them new parameters, we miss the target of flourishing.

It doesn't strike *true*. It is in error.

That doesn't seem so bad if you're at least on the board. Like when you're throwing darts and hit just outside the bullseye. But anything that isn't the truth is false. When we miss the mark, we're shooting at different targets pointed in opposite directions. And it has severe consequences.

Rebellion was born of the serpent. That rebellion in the hands of a person gives birth to sin. And sin gives birth to death. We invent new ways of missing the mark all the time.

The last thing God created was people.

The first thing people created was sin.

And the cycle continues because sin is a virus that consumes its host, and it's always looking for an opportunity to spread. That's why insecurity breeds insecurity.

Have you ever thought about why people make fun of other people? Why we gossip or spread rumors? Why we find a person, or group of people, to be the target of our resentment, rage, frustration, or hate? The root cause of this behavior is insecurity.

We feel the need to prop ourselves up by bringing others down. If we can find some way to diminish someone we identify as a threat or even exploit them as an opportunity to boost our status, perhaps we will feel better about ourselves.

If you've ever been the target of this kind of attack, then …

Tag. You're it.

Someone's insecurity found a new host, and the virus continues to spread. Unless you're aware of it and do something about it, that insecurity will use you to find a new host—whether subtly or aggressively.

Have you ever heard someone who's been called fat share that pain by calling someone else fat? Or ugly? Or stupid? Or worthless? Or slutty? Or a bitch? Or a fag?[19]

I guess it just got real. Those things are illuminated here because they are shared everywhere else. Pain and brokenness are hiding somewhere inside every human, all around you.

You are never more than 20 feet from a person that has been hurt or is hurting. It might even be you. And the feeling of pain finds its comfort in isolation.

We withdraw at different levels. At best, you wear a mask and try to cover up, so no one knows you are wounded. At worst, you eliminate all your relationships and live life in fear and distrust.

Here's the bad news: insecurity doesn't just go away. You can't brush it under the rug. You can't ignore it. You can't pretend it doesn't exist. It has occupied space in your mind with no plans to leave. Perhaps you try to live with it the way you would with an obnoxious roommate. But if you don't draw the line it will continue to take more control. And when your insecurity takes control, it travels. No matter how you might try to contain it, it will slip out of your grasp and find someone nearby. That doesn't mean the things you're insecure about will become the same things other people are insecure about. But what it does mean is that in your efforts to mask your insecurities you will eventually end up elevating yourself above someone else.

When that happens then you've just successfully spread the virus.

Whether you're aware of it or not, you've created insecurities in people. You've done something or said something to someone that has left them feeling naked.

So what do we do? How do we move forward? Is there a solution to this spread of insecurity?

Thankfully the answer is, "Yes."

Which finally brings us to the first question God asks in the Bible:

Where are you?

Hide & Seek

Have you ever found something you didn't know was missing? I'm not talking about finding something you searched for tirelessly only to give up but later come across it. I'm talking about the things that fall between your couch cushions or get kicked under the bed. You find them when you're doing a little tidying up and are only then hit with a short memory of how it got there.

Oh yeah, that popcorn must have been from movie night.

I guess I never donated that free t-shirt from that work thing.

I found a bunch of cords in the closet. I don't know what they go to, so I better keep them in this drawer forever.

We find things all the time we aren't even looking for and don't know we lost. In some cases, finding them becomes a more significant inconvenience than losing them.

I bring that up on the off chance that's how you imagine God thinks about you. People get lost all the time, and occasionally he peels back the sofa cushion of the universe and finds a couple of humans who fell out of his pocket, decaying and collecting dust.

You might even convince yourself you don't think that way in your mind, but some moments feel that way in your heart. Like God forgot you and you're hoping there comes a day he stumbles upon you again.

There are several things we learn about God from the opening pages of the Bible. He is the creator. He is creative. He offers life-giving blessings. He delights in what he has made.

And he notices when you're gone.

When God asks, "Where are you?" it's because he's looking for you. It's because you're on his mind. It's because he wants you back.

You're not the penny that rolled under the sofa. You're the child that's wandered toward the edge of the playground. And your father sees you. He's running over to redirect you to where you need to be—close to him because that's what keeps you safe.

But the reason God is looking for Adam and Eve isn't that he can't find them. He isn't searching for them the way we search for our keys as we scramble to leave for work.

They haven't wandered from God. **They are hiding from him.**

They didn't accidentally stray from his presence. Losing God was intentional. They don't want to be seen, which means ... they don't want to be *found.*

But why would they do such a thing? Why hide from God?

Adam says it was because he was afraid. And he was fearful *because he was naked.*[20]

The same is true for us. Try as we might to cover up our insecurities, deep down we know this doesn't do the trick. We still feel naked. And this feeling does something terrible to us.

It causes us to run and hide from God.

And why do we hide?

Because we're afraid.

And what do we fear?

Judgment.

We will discuss fear and judgment much later in part IV, but it's essential to know this for now:

God establishes his judgment in love, not anger.

Sometimes we imagine when we mess up then God—in his fury—will cast us aside. This story suggests the opposite. When we mess up, we isolate ourselves. We are the ones who hide from God. We don't want to be found.

But that doesn't stop God from searching.

When God asks, "Where are you?" it's because he is on a mission to find the people he created. The people he desires. The people he values. The people he determines can't be replaced.

That means the first question God asks in the Bible gives us some insight into what it means to be human.

To be human is to be desired by God.

To be human is to have inherent value.

To be human is to be irreplaceable.

You may be hiding from God, but he will never stop searching for you.

Fig Leaves & Animal Skins

There is a crucial piece to this story that is sometimes missed.

When Adam and Eve sin and their eyes open, the first thing they do after realizing they're naked is to sew fig leaves together in an attempt to cover up.

But they aren't too confident in their new wardrobe. Even though Adam and Eve do their best to cover themselves, they know their efforts are insufficient.

That's why they hide from God in the first place.

So what does God do when they come out of hiding?
He clothes them.

"And the Lord God made clothing from animal skins for Adam and his wife."[21]

This is the first sacrifice in the Bible. Once again, don't get lost in the logistics and miss the meaning. Here it is:

God makes a sacrifice that covers human shame and insecurity, which allows them to come out of hiding and be who they were meant to be.[22]

It's easy to overlook because it seems like a minor detail, but this is one of the most essential concepts in the entire Scripture library. It gives us a glimpse of God's character immediately after the fall—God clothes human nakedness.

When their efforts don't measure up, when their coverings are insufficient, God does what they are unable to do. When their insecurities dictate that they should hide in the bushes, God clothes them instead.

Why does he do this? Because he is embarrassed or ashamed of their naked bodies?

No. Because *they* are.

There is an infinite list of ways we try to cover up our insecurities. We devote ourselves to our careers; we try to manufacture an image of success and significance; we take extreme efforts to shape and mold our bodies; we target and criticize people who act or think differently than us; we broadcast our accomplishments to the largest possible audience. These efforts all originated from the same place for the same purpose:

They are all ways we cover our insecurity to chase validation.

And the message in this story is clear: they are insufficient. Your shame can't be covered with a handful of fig leaves. You need a different kind of clothing that only God can provide.

God didn't need to cover Adam and Eve to love and embrace them. He did it so they would have the confidence to step out from hiding. He did it so that they would know his love for them and come out of the darkness and into the light. He did it so they would return home where they belonged.

God does this to answer some of *our* questions:

Can God really love me?

Can he really forgive me?

Have I wandered too far?

Have I hidden too well?

We ask these questions when we feel insecure and exposed. They come from the moments we look down and see we're wearing a covering of fig leaves.

These are not new questions. For all of human history, people have asked them. And the answers to these questions don't just come from Genesis.

Two thousand years ago people brought these questions to a wise teacher from Nazareth who understood the mysteries of God and taught with authority.

And to answer these questions, he told a story of a lost son and a heavy robe.

He Came to His Senses

In Luke 15, Jesus tells a few stories that mirror the one we just read; something is missing, and God goes searching.

First a sheep, then a coin, and finally a son. Each of these stories focuses on something of value. Each of these stories has elements of search and celebration. The third story is *The Parable of the Prodigal Son.*

The word prodigal isn't in the story itself, but it was used by the editors of the Bible to describe what was happening. Prodigal means to spend lavishly or even recklessly. Another definition is wastefully extravagant. And when you read the story, you can see why the writer gave the son this description.

Jesus begins by saying there was a father who had two sons and one of them demanded his share of his inheritance. This would customarily be divided with his brother and distributed upon the father's death. It was an incredibly disrespectful request that—to the surprise of the audience—the father granted. Now we know what kind of story we're dealing with.

It is a fairy tale.

No father would grant this son's demand. The same way you wouldn't empty your life savings and hand it to your 16-year-old. It would be irresponsible and unwise. Which is why we should pay attention to the point Jesus is trying to make.

This father is different than we might expect. This father won't exercise authoritative control or use manipulation to negate the son's ambitions.

The Father gives his son the dignity to make his own choices. He isn't a prisoner or a slave. The son is *allowed* to leave home even though it breaks the father's heart.

Jesus is telling us something about God. As human beings made in his image, we are given the dignity of free will. We are permitted to make decisions for ourselves. That means we can make the *wrong* decisions. We can pursue something false.

The first part of the story is predictable. The son goes out to the nearest city, spends his days and nights partying and chasing vanity until—as expected—the money runs out. He loses everything and ends up on the streets. He hits rock bottom when he becomes so hungry he envies what the pigs eat.

It's finally at this moment something changes.

As Jesus tells it, *he came to his senses.*

I guess you could say … **his eyes were opened.** *[wink wink]*

He looked at the consequences of his decisions, and he felt shame at his nakedness.

Sound familiar? It echoes the same ideas presented in the garden—humans recognizing their shame and insecurity and aching for acceptance and renewal.

The son recognized there were better options for him, so he resolved to return home to his father. He knew that his days as a son were over, but perhaps he could hide in the household's shadows somewhere in the background as a servant.

So the son prepared a speech and rehearsed it several times on his journey back home.

I'm sorry. I'm not worthy. I don't deserve to be your son.

As the son neared the house, the father saw him in the distance. I imagine he spent many mornings looking out toward the road, thinking of his son and wondering …

Where are you? [wink wink]

And suddenly, seeing him return, the father was filled with love and compassion. While the son was still a long way off, the father saw him in the distance and ran toward him. It doesn't say in the text, but I imagine this was more than one of those awkward light jogs you have to do when someone is holding the door for you from way too far away.[23] This was one of those sprints where you run so hard your feet almost trip trying to keep up with the pace you've set. He nearly tackles the son and kisses him in a burst of joy and celebration.

Just in case you missed this, there is something worth pointing out:

The father embraces the son *before* his confession.

Sometimes we hold on to our bitterness and resentment until we receive the validation of a confession. When someone has wronged us, we might offer grace and forgiveness on the condition we receive an apology. We want someone to admit we were right, and they were wrong. It's our moment to savor four sweet words that fill us with a sense of affirmation:

I told you so.

Let's try something for a moment. Imagine Jesus was telling this story for the first time, and you were a part of the original audience, but instead of the actual ending, the story ends before the embrace. The son squanders all the family fortunes for a brief taste of luxury and pleasure, realizes his failure, makes his way home, and, as he approaches the house, the father runs after him.

The end.

From your own experience, what would you make of that story? How would you fill in the gaps? How would you reconcile closure? What explanation would you create as to why the father is running toward the son?

I'd probably imagine it was to throw a tightly clasped fist toward his face.

The story has been building to this. The father is about to get his big moment. He will stand in front of a deprived son whose sin and rebellion cost him everything. He will be begging at his father's feet, and the father will get to deliver those same sweet words:

I told you so.

That ending feels a bit more realistic than the one Jesus tells. The ending Jesus tells is nice, but real life isn't full of rainbows and butterflies. We don't tend to forgive like this. We love to say, "I told you so." Sometimes it feels good to have someone indebted to you.

We like it when people recognize their failure and plead for our mercy. We enjoy it when someone tells us:

You were right.

It's not hard to identify why. Because it gives us validation.

And why do we crave validation?

Because we're insecure. Deep down, we're naked, and we know it. And any way we can elevate ourselves begins to feel like protection from vulnerability.

But the father in this story is different from us. The father in this story isn't insecure. He doesn't need to say, "I told you so." And the whole point of this story is to teach us something about God.

God never needs to say, "I told you so," because he isn't insecure. He isn't insecure because he doesn't need validation. God doesn't need anything from you. Let that sink in for a moment.

God doesn't need anything from you.

One more time: God. Doesn't. Need. Anything. From. You.

He doesn't need your worship. He doesn't need your energy. He doesn't need your time. He doesn't need your money. He doesn't need your acknowledgment.

He is Truth. And Truth is eternally secure in the Truth.

That means everything God does is for *your* benefit, not his. He knows that his way is best, but he isn't waiting for us to recognize it. He's running after us and interrupting our confession with his warm embrace because he knows when we come home to him we are where we belong.

If this picture of God is accurate, then we should be *compelled* to follow him because this is goodness beyond anything we've ever seen. This God deserves our worship. He deserves our energy. He deserves our time. He deserves our money. He deserves our acknowledgment.

He doesn't need anything, and so he deserves everything.

A Heavy Robe

The son returns home recognizing his sin, but the father has taken hold of him before he could even utter a word of confession.

That doesn't mean confession is irrelevant.

It is a crucial stage in the journey to return home. It holds tremendous significance. The confession is necessary, but not for the father.

The confession is for the son.

God already knows that his way is best. When we come to our senses and make a confession, we aren't informing God of our error. We're telling ourselves. We speak out a confession so that what has awoken in our hearts will materialize in our actions. God already knows what is best. We confess, so we do, too.

What draws the son back home is the acknowledgment that his way took him on a path toward destruction. That he made a mistake. That changes needed to be made. That he shouldn't govern his life through his own ambition.

It's the same revelation Adam and Eve had in the garden. Their pursuit of becoming like God was their downfall. It only brought shame and despair.

Confession is a demonstration of our awareness that God should decide what is best. That there is error in our ways. That we should not define the good life for ourselves.

Confession is how we come out of hiding and strip off the coverings we've made for ourselves. Confession is when we're standing naked before God—revealing who we truly are—wondering if he could still love us.

And after the son's confession, notice what the Father does …

He clothes him.

"Bring out the finest robe. Put a ring on his finger and sandals on his feet."[24]

In a patriarchal society, which robe do you think would be the finest? The father's.

The father clothes the son in his own robe.

Don't forget, Jesus is telling us this story to teach us something about God. So the question we must ask is, what kind of clothes does God wear? Unless the authors of the Bible forgot to mention the cosmic Gucci store, it's probably safe to assume we aren't talking about threads.

The Psalms are an excellent place to start. They tell us that God is clothed in majesty and strength.[25] They say he wears honor and light.[26] If God is willing to fill our wardrobe with majesty, strength, honor, and light, I think we'd feel pretty good about it.

Look at how Isaiah 61:10 says it:

> I am overwhelmed with joy in the LORD my God! For he has dressed me with the clothing of salvation and wrapped me in a robe of righteousness. I am like a bridegroom dressed for his wedding or a bride with her jewels.

This is a powerful image. You never look better than on your wedding day. And that—according to the biblical authors—is a picture of how God is working to clothe us. He will dress us in honor and proudly present us before all creation as we approach him down the aisle.

This gives us new insight into what God is doing when he clothes Adam and Eve in the garden. This parable of the prodigal son shows us how the father exchanges the son's dirty, ragged clothes for something elegant and beautiful. He is restored to his rightful place as a son, and he looks the part.

When God is clothing Adam and Eve, it's for the same purpose—to restore them to their rightful place as sons and daughters.

God wants us to have the confidence to stand naked before him. That means fully exposing our shame and revealing our insecurity. It's an excruciating and vulnerable step, but the point isn't to stay naked—nor is it to cover ourselves—but to be clothed by God.

And when God clothes us, the result is overwhelming joy. We don't hide behind the bushes; we celebrate like it's a wedding.

These are the clothes that Jesus wears. Which brings us to another question:

Was Jesus Ever Naked?

In a physical sense of the term, the answer is obvious: yes.

Jesus was born in his birthday suit. He had his diapers changed. He bathed. He changed clothes. And perhaps on one of the many occasions he withdrew for a time of solitude, it was also to feel the sun on places it normally doesn't shine.[27]

But what about being spiritually naked? Open and vulnerable before the creator? Hopefully the answer is just as obvious: yes.

The difference is that Jesus never felt the shame and the insecurity. The kind of shame and insecurity that convinces us that we're not good enough. The kind that makes us compare ourselves to others. The kind that generates resentment at our circumstance or status or accomplishments because we've done everything we can and still feel the weight of the pressure to do more.

Jesus never felt the kind of shame and insecurity that makes us rank our status among others. The kind that supplies us with doubts of who we are. The kind where we worship and idolize the people who have the lives we envy and hate and scorn the people we think are below us.

Jesus never felt shame at his nakedness because he never rebelled against God. Jesus never adopted insecurity because he was completely validated in his true identity.

But that doesn't make him unrelatable. On the contrary, Hebrews 4:15 tells us that Jesus, as our High Priest, understood our weaknesses because he faced all the same tests we do, yet he did not sin.[28]

That means Jesus heard the same serpent voice we all hear. The voice that spoke in the garden to Adam and Eve. The voice that encouraged rebellion through coercive doubt.

The voice that makes you wonder …

Did God *really* say …?

According to the Bible, from the beginning of humanity, this voice has been present in every heart and mind. And one by one, it conquered its victims and left them feeling naked and ashamed.

Until Jesus.

The Bible tells us Jesus spent time with God praying and fasting for 40 days and nights when he heard the voice of the tempter in the wilderness.

"If you are the Son of God …."[29]

Did you catch that?

If.

The very statement plants a seed of doubt. Here it is implied that Jesus' identity is only accepted if he can prove something. That he can only become who he was meant to be if he met the conditions and expectations placed on him. In other words, the underlying tones of this temptation are communicating something devastating …

You might not be who you think you are.

This voice attacks the foundation of his identity. If you can get Jesus to question who he is, perhaps you can convince him he's no one. And if you can convince him he's no one, maybe you can convince him he's forgotten, alone, and unloved. And if you can convince him of that, you can entice him with an offer to become someone better through his own effort.

Maybe you can do that … *if* … Jesus doesn't know who he is.

But that's where this story takes a different turn. This story isn't like in the garden. Jesus isn't like Adam.

Adam is much more than a man. Adam is a symbol.[30] Because stories are much more than events—they are ways we find meaning. And that meaning is discovered when we contrast the temptations in the garden with the temptation in the wilderness—the lure of Adam and the temptation of Jesus.

Through Adam, sin and shame entered the world. By doubting God's goodness and breaking the boundary that was set, his eyes were opened, and he saw that he was naked. This rebellion caused him to hide from God and others. This story tells us what we already know: there are insecurities we cover up and hide. If all of our nakedness and shame is traced to its origin, it will link us to the garden's temptation.

We would hear the familiar voice that nudges us to make a kingdom for ourselves because God's way is limiting. He's holding out on us.

But if all those doubts entered the world through one man, they find their end in another.

Jesus is the second Adam. He diverges from the familiar script that has been played out by all of humanity. A script that dictated our failure and weakness. Jesus writes a new story. Unlike Adam, when he hears the voice of doubt—when he is tempted to forget who he is—he doesn't consume the forbidden fruit. He confidently responds …

For it is written.[31]

Meaning there is something else at play. There is another narrative. Jesus isn't left to determine his value isolated and alone. There is a source that informs his perspective. There is a source that stabilizes and grounds him on a solid foundation. There is a source that allows him to identify and dismiss what is false.

This source is *Truth.*

Jesus never felt the naked shame and insecurity of Adam and Eve because he knew the truth. And the truth allows you to see through the hollow barrier of a lie.

Jesus draws from the source of truth, which enables him to dismiss the temptation to question his identity and become susceptible to disobeying God. That's what truth does for all of us.

Notice Jesus claims this statement in the present tense. He doesn't say, "For it was written." Jesus isn't clinging to some ancient philosophy hoping it holds up for his day. What was the truth then is the truth now. For Jesus, this source of truth is alive and breathing life back into him.

From Genesis to Matthew to today, the truth has always been there.

For it is written …

Imagine how short the Bible would be if Adam and Eve clung to God's truth and trusted in what he told them. The serpent would try to plant that same seed of doubt.

Did God really say ...?

Yep. The end.

That's why Jesus changes everything. He didn't allow that temptation to make him question his identity. He knew who he was because he trusted who God was. If God tells you that you are made in his image, through his love, for a great purpose, and you wholeheartedly believe it without a shadow of a doubt, then you're no longer ashamed when you stand naked before him.

As a result, God covers you in righteousness. God clothes you with security and peace.

That's what Jesus came to do. He came to find us in the places we're hiding and clothe us in his righteousness. Because he knows the truth. *For it is written.*

This is why we need to be aware of the voices speaking to us. We all hear voices of doubt or criticism or shame. We all hear the voices that make us question our value or our potential. We all hear the voices that mock our dreams or confront our ability to achieve them.

These are the voices that bring insecurity, and insecurity keeps us from becoming everything we were meant to be.

Sometimes these voices are external. Other times they come from within. Either way, it's important to make this declaration: they are false.

But here's the problem: how do you know what is truth and what is a lie? Especially when the lie is always trying to cover the truth.

Jesus addresses this problem in Matthew 7. He claims,

Anyone who listens to my teaching and follows it is wise, like a person who builds a house on solid rock. Though the rain comes in torrents and the floodwaters rise, and the winds beat against that house, it won't collapse because it is built on bedrock. But anyone who hears my teaching and doesn't obey it is foolish, like a person who builds a house on sand. When the rains and floods come and the winds beat against that house, it will collapse with a mighty crash.[32]

According to Jesus, building a life on his teaching and following his way is standing on a firm foundation of truth.

How do you identify a lie? Anything that isn't of Jesus.

All those lies are a foundation of sand. But the truth of Jesus will hold up.

Jesus never felt naked the way Adam and Eve felt naked. The way we feel naked. He wasn't ashamed or insecure. He didn't try to cover or hide. He stood on the solid foundation of truth, and he was able to be who he was meant to be.

What Ever Happened to Lazarus?

Even though Jesus was secure in the truth, he still grieved.

The Bible tells us he was a man acquainted with sorrow.[33] Our wandering and rebellion came at a high cost, and Jesus paid the price.

It's *because* Jesus was secure in the Truth that he experienced grief.

And why did Jesus grieve?

Because of his love.

Grief is intimately connected to the things that fill our hearts and garner our affections. If we were indifferent toward something or someone, they wouldn't have the power to impact our emotions. Our grief is tied to something we care for, and it is expressed when it has been harmed in some way.

We grieve the loss of a loved one. We grieve the loss of a job. We grieve the loss of a relationship. We grieve the decisions our children make. We grieve our disappointments. We grieve a dream we once had. We grieve change.

All of these things are fueled by our investment of hope, love, and desire.

The shortest verse in the Bible is two words, and they are found in John 11. Jesus got word from concerned family members that Lazarus was in critical condition. He and his disciples made it to them after traveling for three days, but it was too late.

Lazarus died.

Jesus wept.[34]

Books have been filled with the significance of these two words. Debates argued. Theologies formed. Among the number of the things to consider that shape our understanding of what is taking place here, this can indeed be true—Jesus cares deeply.

And when you care for something that is harmed, you grieve.

Moments before Jesus weeps, he makes a significant statement. As he is speaking with Martha, he tells her:

> I am the resurrection and the life. Anyone who believes in me will live, **even after dying.** Everyone who lives in me and believes in me will never die.[35]

What an interesting statement. He says this *before* he weeps.

Why does Jesus do this? If he knows everything is going to be made right, why does he succumb to such a dramatic emotion?

That's a pretty loaded question, and it's impossible to provide a simple answer. Wrestling with this concept is like attempting to gather the mind of God and fit it into the confines of our understanding.

We are too limited.

So what do you do with this? What do you do with your messiah—your God—crying by the side of a tomb, right after he said you would never die? When he's secure in the truth but still *feeling* the hurt?

Do we even have a category for that? I'm glad I exist on this side of the resurrected Jesus because I don't think I could have handled this moment in person. Of all the things you could witness, God weeping isn't one that inspires confidence.

Until Lazarus comes out of the tomb.

I guess the whole weeping thing was some sort of a dramatic abstract intermission? Perhaps Jesus was looking to add an Oscar to his mantle with this theatrical performance?

Whatever you make of the weeping episode, all is made right, and celebration ensues.

I'm not sure what happened that day. I don't know what people said or thought or felt. But there is one thing I do know.

Even though it isn't written in the Bible, Lazarus later died *again.*

I think that is sometimes missed in this story. We are drawn to the miracle of Jesus raising someone from the dead. That deserves our attention and curiosity. But what the story doesn't tell us is—despite how Lazarus felt in his newly awakened body for however long his life was extended—that body eventually failed. And he died *again.*

Because the problem remains.

We are all going to die.

Even the ones that die and come back to life.

That's because there is still a felt tension in this world. It's not yet fully restored.

When Jesus performed miracles and healed the sick, it gathered crowds and expanded the community of people astonished by Jesus. The men and women who felt the surge of Jesus' healing power rush through their body and eliminate their illness surely felt a shot of excitement and gratitude. They left the scene with a new outlook on life. They told their family, friends, and neighbors of the man from Nazareth who brought healing.

And as time passed, they, too, returned to dust.

Among the reasons Jesus wept, this is undoubtedly one of them:

Death is *still* claiming territory and hurting what God loves and cares for deeply.

The Curse of Time

I had an epiphany where this all made more sense to me when I became a father. After my son was born, everything in my life changed. I had to shift my schedule; I had to reorder my priorities; I had to make new sacrifices.

And it was all worth it.

It was a joy to me. I felt truly blessed to be entrusted to care for this person that entered the world. On my son's first birthday, I wanted to get him a gift. Not something that he would outgrow or that would eventually make its way into the trash. I wanted to give him something that would hopefully increase in value and have deep meaning in his life.

So I wrote him a letter.[36]

He won't be reading it any time soon. But that's the point. It is a collection of thoughts and ideas and prayers and dreams that trace the pattern of his life and vision for his future. The same is true of the ones I write to my daughter.[37]

As my son's second birthday was approaching, I began preparing to write his next letter. But before I did, I wanted to go back and reread the first birthday letter to remember the events of his first year of life. I pulled out the sheet from its envelope, sat down on the couch of a vacant living room, and began to read. And as I read …

I wept.

This brought me new insight into the moment when Jesus heard the news of his friend Lazarus.

As I processed my emotion, I was able to identify its source. It was a combination of two things: gratitude and sorrow. Allow me to explain each one.

Reading the letter gave me an overwhelming sense of gratitude. I was reminded of the important events that stood out. I will never forget the memories that defined the year. It was an exciting time because everything was new. First smile. First word. First step. I felt like I dove headfirst into the moments that taught me how beautiful and enjoyable life can be. A flood of joy rushed over me, and by the time I got to my signature, I was drowning. I couldn't help but say, *"Thank you."*

Thank you, God, for my child. Thank you for the moments I got to witness. Thank you for entrusting him to me.

We say, "Thank you," when we're grateful.

But the feeling of gratitude was merged with a sense of sorrow. It rushed in just as fast as the joy once I realized one thing:

That year is gone.

I'll never get it back. It was so beautiful and life-changing and *good.* And now something good is *gone.*

After reading the letter, I mourned the loss of experiences that came only once. It wasn't because I wasted the year or took it for granted. I didn't feel sorry because I was reckless with the opportunities I had. It was a year of intentionality like none I had ever invested. I soaked up every moment with my new growing family.

It was because I was so intentional that year that I felt sorrow. It was the creation of something good, and any time something good is lost or gone, it is cause to grieve. After the feeling settled in, I realized I prayed something else to God …

Help.

Help me, God, with my child. Help me take advantage of the moments I have with him. Help me live a life worthy of this gift.

We seek help when we feel sorrow.

I can only speculate, but my weeping moment gave me a sense these same emotions were present within Jesus while he broke down near the tomb.

Gratitude and sorrow.

This is so good. This is so painful.

I can't believe I had this. I can't believe it's gone.

I want this to last forever. The end has come.

Thank you, God. Help me, God.

When we examine our lives and evaluate our pursuit of meaning, we do so realizing we are limited by one thing …

Time.

It often sits at the top of a list outlining our commodities. You may have heard or said that time is valuable or even precious.

That isn't true.

We only say that because it is the governing power that holds possession of the things that are precious to us. If you say your time is valuable, it's only because it contains the thing you value.

If time itself was valuable, we'd all spend our time watching a clock tick away. And of course, you wouldn't do that because it would be a *waste* of time.

And why would it be a waste? Because the actual valuable thing was getting away from you.

The reality is, the things you love are getting away from you because of the tyranny of time.

This is a curse of the fall. When death entered the world, it introduced us to the concept of time. The universe had a beginning. And because of sin, it will have an end. When Jesus was born into the world, he accepted mortality. One way or another, he was destined to die.

You don't *have* time. Time has *you.* And it is meticulously counting down to the moment it will take everything away.

No one understood this better than Jesus. He knew the value of his human creation. He knew their potential. He knew the image they bore that had been covered by sin. And most importantly, he knew how to reclaim it all. His comprehension of what was lost gave him a clear vision to accomplish God's mission.

Jesus knew the beauty of this life. Jesus knew the tragedy of our death.

Jesus wept.

In-between the balance of these polarizing realities is an invitation.

Which path will you take? Will you allow yourself to be rescued, or will you refuse? It's an important question. One that everyone should consider.

And while you're thinking about how you will fill your life-moments, make sure you don't kill time because time is killing you.

So what should we be spending our time doing?

The Flesh

We all have things that we want—unfulfilled desires. Some of the things we desire are good. But some of them aren't. Why do we chase after something we know is wrong?

It's because the voice of doubt doesn't stop whispering in our ears. It entices us in ways that appeal to our insecurities. And because our insecurities create powerful desires, it's hard to say, "No."

This is what we call temptation.

We all need to be aware of the temptations we face. Temptation, by its very nature, is a promise to satisfy a desire within us. That is why it is so appealing. Because it seems to bring a reward that fulfills something we crave.

And guess what?

It's true.

Whatever tempts you *will* fulfill the desire for something you crave. Sinful or otherwise. We need to come clean about a myth that has been created about sin. Often you hear people say that sin won't fulfill you. That's not exactly true.

What's true is that it won't fulfill you for very long.

When you indulge in your sinful cravings, you will satisfy them for a short time—just like when you get hungry and eat a big meal. The hunger will subside, but it will creep back up again later.

Let's get very specific to understand how this works. If you hear someone say chasing fame or sex or money or (fill in the blank) isn't satisfying, what they probably mean is that it isn't *ultimately* fulfilling in the long run.

It doesn't gratify all your needs as a human. It may satisfy one need and negate several others. It might check off a few boxes, but it leaves a lot blank. Satisfying some of these needs might mean neglecting—or even starving—others. If it isn't *ultimately* fulfilling, then it misses the mark.

And missing the mark of life to the full is ultimately death.

The problem isn't that you won't feel fulfilled. **The problem is that you will.** The problem is that you will feel filled by something that isn't ultimately fulfilling.

But only for a short time. You will think your desires have been gratified, but you are left empty. And when the hunger returns, you'll return to the source that convinces you you're fed. And the more you feed it, the more it grows.

The Bible calls this hunger *the flesh.* When we think of flesh, we likely think about our bodies because our bodies are made of flesh. But this doesn't quite capture what the Bible is describing.

A great definition of the flesh is our "disordered desires."[38]

Let's look back at the garden. When God gave Adam and Eve boundaries, it was to protect them. Here is something worth saying, because it's where so many people get stuck.

Throughout the Bible, God never prohibits something good.

Often we think God's boundaries and commands are to keep us repressed. They are set up to prevent us from having fun and enjoying life. But this is never true. God never withholds anything good. If he is providing a command or setting up a boundary it's to keep you away from danger and destruction.

The issue is that as a result of our sin and shame, the things we desire are out of whack. Our vision is skewed, and now we can't truly see.

Unhealthy Eyes

For a long time, I had terrible vision, but I had no idea. I have only ever had my vision, so I had nothing to compare it to.

Until one day, I missed my exit on the highway. My wife asked why I didn't move over, and I explained it was because I couldn't read the exit sign until it was too late. Then she started testing my vision by asking me to read signs up ahead.

"Can you read that one?"

I was convinced the sign she referred to was 18 miles away. No human could read the sign she was pointing to. Few telescopes were up to the challenge.

But I was wrong. She told me what it said. And I was able to confirm it, but only when I was about 15 feet away.

I needed glasses.

Which I got a week later. I remember the first time I tried them on. It was like seeing in high definition. I had no idea my vision was so poor because it was what I had become so accustomed to. If I could have compared it to my eyesight from about 15 years earlier, I would have noticed the difference instantly.

But because my vision became impaired gradually, I didn't notice something concerning had developed.

This is the obstacle Jesus identifies for all of us. Our disordered desires of the flesh are deeply connected to our vision. They grip us when we spend more and more time staring at the wrong things.

Our eyes become fixated, and it has a huge impact.

> *Your eye is like a lamp that provides light for your body. When your eye is healthy, your whole body is filled with light. But when your eye is unhealthy, your whole body is filled with darkness.*[39]

When our eyes lock onto the wrong things, it brings destruction to our whole wellbeing.

This is what happened in Genesis. The entire fall of humans began with the eyes. As Eve considered taking the fruit, it says,

> *So when the woman saw that the tree was good for food, **and that it was a delight to the eyes**, and that the tree was to be desired to make one wise, she took of its fruit and ate.*[40]

Unhealthy eyes fixate on the wrong things. And what is the result?

Desire.

This word for desire comes from the Hebrew word *chamad.*

Chamad is later used in Exodus in one of the commandments. When God is directing the community of his people, he says you shall not *chamad* "your neighbor's house. You shall not *chamad* your neighbor's wife, his male or female servant, his ox or donkey, or anything that belongs to your neighbor."[41]

Chamad here is translated as covet.

To covet is to experience a longing for something you don't have. To look out the window and yearn for the things you don't possess. We covet with our eyes because we covet what we see. What we stare at.

Hannibal Lector uses this concept to aid in the capture of Buffalo Bill, a sadistic serial killer in *The Silence of the Lambs.* Speaking to agent Clarice Starling, Lector says, "He covets. That is his nature. And how do we begin to covet, Clarice? Do we seek out things to covet? No. We begin by coveting what we see every day."[42]

Chamad is married to temptation because we are only tempted by the things we desire, and we always want the things we covet.

When we look out to the world, we will see all kinds of things that will entice us. When we stare at things that are good for us, our whole body will be full of light. That sounds encouraging. But regardless of your worldview, you will agree that there are many things out there that aren't good for us.

Staring at these things makes our eyes unhealthy.

And here is a warning:

If you stare at something terrible for you long enough, you will be convinced it's right. And when you think something bad for you is good for you, then you're truly lost.

Jesus is talking about something we all do. It's called …

Justification.

There are times when we all look at something we initially know we shouldn't. But the longer we stare, the more we begin to justify why it's not only permissible for us but *good.* Let's use an affair as an example.

Say you're in a struggling marriage (or even just had a bad couple of days), and a temptation approaches you. Maybe you pick up on a subtle flirtatious comment from a coworker or go so far as to create a login profile for online dating—or hookup—site.

This stage ignites your curiosity. You're simply wondering what is within your reach, so you chase these things a little further down the path.

Let's say you chase them far enough to an actual invitation. Now your options aren't hypothetical. They are reaching out to you. You go from curiosity to consideration. And as you're considering this new opportunity, you're asking yourself questions.

Don't I deserve love? Shouldn't I be happy? If no one finds out, what's the harm?

Soon you'll cross a line from consideration to negotiation. That's when you've already made your decision, and now you have to reason with yourself to get to the point of …

Justification.

An affair is just one example. We walk through these progressions with all kinds of things. Maybe you've been shopping and find something you want that isn't in the budget. How did it end up in your possession?

Curiosity, consideration, negotiation, and, finally, justification.

Do you see the danger in this? If you fix your eyes on something long enough, you could justify anything.

And a world full of people that can justify anything is a world full of murder, rape, corruption, racism, sex trafficking, lying, stealing, abandonment. You get the picture.

Because it's the world you live in. A world you see every day.

That's why Jesus finished with this haunting claim. He concludes, "If the light you think you have is actually darkness, how deep that darkness is!"[43]

Don't forget: humans are thinking creatures. When you look at someone who has done something atrocious, you might feel the urge to label them as a monster. The way you reconcile the existence of such a person is to put them in a unique category of someone who can't think or feel. We want to believe we could never become like them. That the bad things we do aren't as bad by comparison.

But the problems in our society aren't merely the result of people enslaved to primal animal cravings and indifferent instincts. The horrible things humans do are tied to rationalization, logic, and reason.

Each and every person finds a way to justify their actions.

This is a sobering thought because it confronts us with the possibility that we are all capable of doing the same things.

Have you ever looked at something horrible a person has done and thought *I could never do that?*

Yes, you could.

If given the right combination of circumstance and opportunity, any able-bodied human is capable of absolutely anything.

But there is a difference between what you could do and what you would do.

And that difference hinges on what your eyes are staring at.

It remains true that you wouldn't do certain bad things because those aren't the things you want right now.

But if you wanted them—and if you stared long enough—you could give in.

You could justify it. You could become just like the people you label as vastly different from you because we all follow the same pattern.

Curiosity, consideration, negotiation, justification.

And if you get to the point that you can justify something as good when it isn't, that the dark thing within you is light, then how deep that darkness is. Make sure you're getting your eyes checked. What you stare at determines what you desire.

Back Again at the Charcoal Fire

Jesus creates a group of students called disciples. This word comes from the Greek word *mathétés,* which basically means apprentice. Jesus is on a mission to get these people desiring the right things and looking in the right places.

These people weren't considered academic or social elites. Fishermen, tax collectors, former revolutionaries, and everything in-between form this body of students.

These apprentices don't seem to be anything special. Just your average guys trying to make a living. But over time, training under Jesus starts to transform them. They learn the Scriptures. They perform miracles. They cast out demons. They demonstrate their commitment by leaving everything behind and giving everything up. Their possessions. Their careers. Even their families, which were their means for securing a future.

But they all decided it was worth it. Not just because Jesus was an incredible teacher, but because they began to enjoy an elevated life. They became recognizable in the community, and some anticipated that Jesus might become king. The people were hoping to rally together and revolt against the Roman government. And who would they select to lead them?

Jesus, the rabbi.

The man that teaches with wisdom and harnesses the power of God. And if Jesus is made king, who will make up his court?

The disciples.

The people that have been apprenticing under him the past several years. These guys began to imagine a future of prosperity. They even started to debate who would get the highest position when Jesus was coronated.[44]

Among them was Peter, a disciple who vowed his undying devotion. In Matthew 26:35, he tells Jesus, "Even if I have to die with you, I will never disown you."

It's an extreme sentiment, but which one will Jesus promote in the new kingdom? The one that professes his undying loyalty.

By all indications, things were moving up and to the right. People were following Jesus by the thousands. Every day it became harder and harder to travel because of the level of celebrity this group enjoyed. It was like a gold rush, and the people that were there first would certainly reap the benefits. It would have been like being on staff at Apple when the company went public in 1980. The company was on the rise. Projections were good. It seemed like a lock. Until tensions in the company rose, and Steve Jobs resigned.

Everything was good … until it wasn't.

When the religious leaders found a way to arrest Jesus and partner with the Roman government to have him executed, the disciples' dreams of power and position dissolved, and they all fled.

Including Peter.

But it was fear, not disloyalty, that caused him to run. From a distance, Peter followed his shackled rabbi, watching how the events would unfold.

As he inched his way forward, a woman asked him, "You're not one of that man's disciples, are you?"

"No," he told her. "I am not."[45]

The man that claimed he would die for Jesus later proclaims he doesn't even know him. In fact, on two more occasions, he is confronted by people that recognize him, and he does the same thing.

Peter denies Jesus three times.

> Because it was cold, the household servants and the guards had made a **charcoal fire**. They stood around it, warming themselves, and Peter stood with them, warming himself.[46]

Peter is observing the events as they unfold, trying to blend in with the crowd. He can feel the cold breeze in the night air and naturally is drawn to the charcoal fire in front of him. Everyone is huddled around the fire … and Peter is there, too.

In any story, the setting is essential. Space, where the events take place, is a crucial element in how they unfold. When Peter goes against his word and fails to remain loyal to Jesus, he is staring into it.

The charcoal fire.

When your leader is on the chopping block, you're confronted with a tough decision. Self-preservation is a foundational instinct, and if you stick your neck out for the person on trial, you'll feel the cold steel of the ax as it falls.

It might be better to update your resume and try something new. For Peter, the stakes are higher. It wasn't just a career fading away; his life was on the line. We've all said there are things we'd die for, and if you're reading this now, you've either never been confronted with them, or you actually have felt the raw terror that Peter felt that night.

After the death of Jesus, all of the disciples were forced to reconcile their disappointment and adjust to the events that transpired. That meant creating a new plan for their future.

For Peter, it meant trying to bury the shame of the night Jesus was arrested and move on with his life.

We all make mistakes. But some are too shameful to confront. We think it's best to try to forget.

But that isn't the end of the story. At the end of John's gospel, we get one more glimpse of Peter after Jesus is resurrected from the dead. He's back out at sea with some of the other disciples fishing from a boat. Jesus is on shore, but they can't quite see him. He calls out to throw their nets to the other side, and the disciples catch more than they can haul in. At once, they know what's going on, and Peter—in Forest Gump fashion—dives into the water to swim to shore in a rush to get to Jesus first.

The others arrive, and they approach Jesus to discover he has breakfast waiting for them.

And it was cooking over …

A charcoal fire.[47]

This setting is familiar. The last time Peter was standing next to a charcoal fire, he was denying Jesus. And now he is back again— literally confronted with a visual reminder of his failure.

As he stares into the coals, Jesus asks him an important question.

"Do you love me, Peter?"

The tone is difficult to interpret through writing, and that's certainly true when the text is 2,000 years old. Maybe your mind wants you to read this question like Jesus is asking,

"Do you actually love me, Peter?"

As if the words were soaked with doubt and skepticism. This kind of interpretation would lead us to believe the question is rhetorical. It would be like he's asking, "How could you love me if you denied me?"

But Jesus isn't searching for a crack in Peter's spiritual foundation. He isn't spotlighting a weakness in Peter's character. He's extending an invitation.

"Do you love me? Then feed my sheep."

Jesus asks this question three times. **One for each time Peter denied him.** Be assured; this is no coincidence. The author is telling us something important. Jesus doesn't question Peter's love to punish or mock him. It's not from a posture of condemnation or criticism.

Jesus asks if Peter loves him three times because, for every instance of failure, there are as many invitations to return to his true calling.

What if Peter denied four times? Then Jesus would ask four times. Or a hundred. Or a thousand.

And each time Jesus asks, "Do you love me?" it will be accompanied by invitation …

Feed my sheep.

Don't miss the underlying message behind this. Jesus doesn't want to let your failure rob you of your identity.

This question is for Peter, but it's also for us.

Do you love me? Then feed my sheep.

And Jesus asks this question in a precise setting. Peter is now back again at the charcoal fire. The last time he saw this picture, he was making the biggest mistake of his life. This is intentional.

Jesus meets us in the place of our greatest shame to give us our most magnificent redemption.[48]

We might want to run from the charcoal fire—out of sight out of mind. When it comes to our mistakes and failures we'd rather resolve them internally. Fashion some fig leaves and cover them up. It's easier to tell ourselves to do better and never have to take responsibility for our actions.

But for the sake of our emotional and spiritual renewal, Jesus refuses to allow us to brush it under the rug or hide it behind a bush. He brings us back to the settings of our shame—not to condemn—but to restore. The first time Peter was at the charcoal fire, he felt alone. The second time, Jesus was with him.

But this part is crucial so don't miss it …

Jesus doesn't want you to revisit your failures as a punishment. He wants to expose your failures to make progress. He wants you to stand naked before him and target the shame and insecurity that's forcing you into hiding.

It's not to lay on you a heavy burden. It's to free you from unnecessary baggage. Jesus doesn't want to create a feeling of guilt. He wants you to feel the grace within his gift: a new tomorrow.
A better tomorrow. One where we turn from our vices and live in God's peace.

Jesus brings us back to the charcoal fire to ignite our hope. Hope that Jesus is greater than our failures.

If you've been looking for Jesus but haven't been able to find him, consider heading toward the charcoal fire. It's the source of your shame and insecurity. That's where Jesus is waiting for you. He's cooking breakfast and has time to talk.

Clothed in a Cross [Necklace]

Jesus wants to transform the images of our shame into images of victory.

That's what he did with the cross. Before his execution, the cross was a symbol used for political manipulation. It was a reminder of how powerless you were to oppose the strength of the system. It was an image that inspired fear and diminished ambitions of rebellion. The cross was a symbol of shame.

Was.

Now it has a very different meaning. When someone wears a cross, it's not to invoke a feeling of shame; it's to inspire hope. It's a reminder of God's saving power. It is a message to the authorities and principalities that there is a true king who governs with love, grace, and truth.

The message of the cross spread with the whispers of people rebelling against fear. And they didn't stay whispers for long. That's why we're still talking about Jesus today. He flipped the script on the symbol that once stood for oppression, fear, and grief.

Jesus wants to do the same thing with the symbols of your most profound shame. He wants to turn the things that represent your most significant failures into your proudest success. He will bury your mistakes in the grave, and they will become seeds for new life.

It sounds too good to be true, right?

That's why so many of us refuse to let these symbols leave our grip. That's why we hold on to the memories that haunt us. That's why we adopt false identities. That's why we believe the lies about who we are.

When we hold on to the pain and bitterness and resentment, it connects us to what we lost.

Even some of Jesus' disciples wrestled with doubt. When they saw the cross, they saw death as the winner and another victory of the broken system. Many of us take the same posture with the symbols of our shame.

We let them have power over us.

But imagine if our jewelry bore the images of our former shame; what would those necklaces look like?

A money sign? A porn distributor logo? A liquor bottle? A family name? A picture of someone we've hurt?

We might feel embarrassed to advertise the shame of our past, but that is what God wants us to do. We may not wear it like jewelry, but we show it in our witness. Jesus invites you to walk the path of your most profound shame or worst mistake to return to who you really are.

This process cannot be manipulated or coerced. To see and experience true restoration, our posture must be authentic. We must allow God to meet us in our places of shame and regret— not to dwell in the guilt of our mistakes—but to take us by the hand and lead us on a different path.

The Preacher and the Prostitute

Every so often, I have this dream that I go out in public and realize I forgot to get dressed. Some people have this dream in the form of going to school in their underwear.

If only I was so lucky.

Every time I have a dream like this, I am completely naked. The entire dream is spent trying to hide or cover-up. For some reason, I never simply leave the setting—or wake up, for that matter. Instead, I remain engaged with my surroundings and try to pass off that I'm not naked.

But regardless of my tactics in the dream, and no matter who I fool, I am still acutely aware of my predicament. I am restless, uncomfortable, and anxious.

Maybe it's just a weird dream. Or perhaps it's telling me something.

Even though I've never actually forgotten to leave home without first getting dressed, I have felt this same unnerving tension while awake. There are moments when I sense I am exposed, and my preferred method of camouflage is to attempt to blend in. The problem, of course, is even if I am successful and no one notices, I am trapped in the awareness of my vulnerability.

Every interaction is spent somehow trying to cover up or hide. You always know when you're vulnerable, even if the people around you don't. They might be firing live rounds, unaware that you've stumbled into the gun range, hiding behind a paper target.

This happens in all sorts of ways.

Molding your opinions to accommodate your group of friends. Keeping silent when you observed something questionable in the workplace. Doing something that makes you uncomfortable to please someone. Compromising your morals to get ahead.

Just blend in. Don't let them know what you're thinking.

Every time we do this, we're constructing a covering of fig leaves and grabbing anything in reach to cover ourselves. And if that isn't enough—and it rarely is—then we can just resort to hiding behind the bush.

Some people might cover themselves with humor or sarcasm. Some might cover with anger. Some might cover with fear. Some might cover with confidence. Some might cover with work. Some might play defense, and some might go on the attack.

None of us want to feel exposed, and we all find ways to cover whatever makes us feel vulnerable or insecure.

That's one of the main reasons we criticize. It's easier to hide in the stands than to stand on the field.

Haven't you ever heard someone screaming at an athlete on television with an exhaustive evaluation of how terrible they are at their sport? We have casual conversations about professional athletes and throw out phrases like "they suck," as if they'd cower in fear to face us on the field.[49]

That's why it's so hard to put yourself out there. You have seen so many people face the firing squad of criticism. Maybe you've even lined up your sights and pulled the trigger on someone else yourself.

Haven't you read the comments section lately?

We live in a digital world of unsolicited interaction and engagement, and it's easy to contribute your opinion even when no one is asking for it. Merely typing a few words can light a match under a river of gasoline. Unfortunately, some people just want to see others burning with self-doubt and insecurity.

And where does that desire come from?

Their own insecurity.

Because, like we've already discussed, insecurity breeds insecurity. Anyone that needs to spend their time verbally abusing other people is merely trying to mask their insecurities.

And eventually, insecurity will morph into …

Contempt.[50]

Contempt is simply considering yourself better than someone else. It's the feeling that someone is worthless or to be pitied. It's how we justify exercising disgust toward a person without feeling remorse or guilt—we convince ourselves that it's deserved.

Perhaps you've felt contempt toward a criminal. Maybe a murderer or a thief or a rapist. We certainly look down upon the kinds of people that do such offensive acts. But our circle of contempt expands much further than these extreme categories. Maybe you've felt contempt for someone in dire circumstances like a pregnant teen, a homeless person, or someone addicted to drugs.

Our pride gives us permission to look down on such individuals.

If you stop there then you're certainly better than me. I've weaponized contempt and become trigger happy. To my great shame, I've caught myself feeling contempt toward people for every reason imaginable. For the way people look, act, dress, their hobbies, their jobs, their education, their athletic ability, their strengths, their weaknesses, their family, their approach to parenting, the way they spend money, their religion, their worldview, their mannerisms, their social media accounts … the list, heartbreakingly, goes on.

When I look at this list, I don't just see words. I see people. Or should I say—by God's grace—I see people. And I genuinely think I can tell myself …

I'm better than them.

When I take a moment to speak this aloud, I realize I'm not disgusted with any of these people.

I'm disgusted with myself.

I am embarrassed to admit I have felt, and occasionally still feel, contempt for another human being. But all of this is simply a tower I have built, and if I trace each emotion, I can get to the root of the problem. We simply have to slow down and ask,

Why do I feel this way?

I'll answer for myself.

I feel contempt because I think I'm better than someone. I think I'm better than someone because I desire to elevate myself above them. I desire to promote myself because I am terrified of feeling insignificant. I'm terrified of feeling insignificant because I'm insecure.

And … *[drumroll, please]* …

I'm insecure because I feel shame at my nakedness.

This is how we justify contempt, but it all stems back to the original problem.

We are running from God and trying to cover ourselves up. And contempt is just one way we hide our insecurities.

This is not only wrong, but it keeps us in the isolation of the ivory tower where we imprison ourselves. You can't form meaningful relationships with others or make a positive contribution to the world if you live your life thinking you're better than everyone.

That's when it hit me.

Deep down, we're all the same. We're all trying to make our way in life, searching for meaning, truth, beauty, and love. And we're all hiding behind the layers we put on because we're afraid it might be out of reach.

In other words, the preacher and the prostitute are searching for the same thing.

They are both searching for meaning, beauty, truth, and love. They are both searching for a rich and satisfying life. We all are.

The only difference between them is they are searching for it in different places. And where we search for the good in life will ultimately determine the people we become.

You can't help anyone you view with contempt.

Jesus didn't have contempt for anyone. He just came to help people find what they had been looking for the whole time.

East of Eden

I spend a lot of time comparing myself to other people.

Even as I write this book, I compare myself to the authors I admire and respect. It's not all bad. Some comparisons can be a catalyst for growth.

But comparison will always eventually become toxic. You will start to devote your time and energy and affection to a life that doesn't belong to you. You'll want to be someone else. You'll want what someone else has. Their accomplishments. Their possessions. Their relationships. Their opportunities.

Comparison is always aimed at contentment. We imagine if we have what they have then we will be happy.

The comparison will convince you it's a pathway, but it's a prison. It's the very thing keeping you from the contentment you desire. It's the feeling you don't have enough; you haven't done enough …

You'll never *be* enough.

We're afraid who we are doesn't measure up. That means when we compare ourselves, what we're chasing is …

Validation.

I matter. I'm significant. I'm valued. I'm thought of. I'm seen. I'm gifted. I'm unique.

I'm loved.

The truth is, you need validation. But where can you find it?

If you seek validation from the world, you'll never grab hold of it. It's like trying to capture smoke in your hand—it will always evade your grip. That's because the comparison is never satisfied. You'll always find someone to make you feel inferior.

But when we seek validation from God, you learn you *already have it.*

"God showed his great love for us by sending Christ to die for us **while we were still sinners.**"[51]

This is how God validates you. This verse is saying that before you ever accomplished anything, before you ever reached any goal, before you ever tried to improve yourself,

God said …

You matter. You're significant. You're valued. You're thought of. You're seen. You're gifted. You're unique.

You're loved.

This is how God clothes you. A sacrifice is made—while we were still sinners—so we can exchange our fig leaves for animal skins. It's the story of Adam and Eve. It's the story of us.

And this story seems to have a happy ending. Until you read the next verse.

This is what happens in Genesis *after* God clothes Adam and Eve …

"So the Lord God banished them from the Garden of Eden …."[52]

Wait … what?

What about all that "God clothing them" stuff? I thought things were good? Why is God suddenly kicking them out?

God's clothing is a sign of his love, but a reminder that something is hiding underneath. We are still in a fallen state.

When we're talking about feeling naked we're talking about a condition. We're talking about a universal tension we experience regardless of how many layers we're wearing. This isn't about how comfortable you may or may not be streaking through the quad.

This is about dismantling your insecurity the only way that works — exposing it before God and allowing him to clothe you in healing, renewal, and validation.

We were created to be naked before God. We were created to be fully confident in who he made us to be. We were created to fix our eyes on him and live in continuous unity with his will.

Being naked before God is a good thing …

But it doesn't *feel* that way.

And why is that?

Because we are still broken people in a broken world. There is no easy fix to shame and insecurity. It's a difficult process to trust in the love, grace, and validation God is offering.

No one wants to stand naked and exposed, but standing naked and exposed is the way toward reaching your full potential.

Does that mean you will one day be frolicking, literally, in the nude through sunflower fields when you step foot in God's eternal kingdom?

Honestly, I don't know. But what I do know is this:

You won't feel naked the way you do now. You won't feel the urge to hide your shame or mask your insecurity — because it won't exist. The work God is doing is to fully restore you to your true self.

There is a challenging road ahead, and any journey we're traveling is a clear reminder: we aren't at home. We are east of Eden. We haven't arrived at our destination.

The banishment of Adam and Eve is a mercy given to all of us — a maneuver of compassion. God will not allow us to live forever in a fallen state. God wants to escort us back into his kingdom. Into the garden where we can eat from the tree of life.

And so we need to come out from hiding, shed our handmade fig leaf coverings, and present ourselves naked before God, ready to be clothed from his sacrifice.

There is a lot of work to be done. And the work begins now, with you. With where you're at. Or maybe a better way of putting it is …

What you're …

PART II

IN

|*in*| |IN|
Preposition, Adverb

1   Positioned inside or within the limits of something, or contained, surrounded, or enclosed by something: *The cup is in the cabinet, John was in prison, etc.*

2   Being a member or forming a part of something: *Do you like cream in your coffee? Mrs. Johnson is in a meeting, etc.*

3   Experiencing a situation, condition, or feeling: *Have you ever been in love? We watched in horror as the cars crashed, etc.*

Not *in* Kansas Anymore

I went to a small Christian university in Indiana, so it was part of my contract to get married right out of college. I was surrounded by hundreds of women wanting a proposal and hundreds of men competing for their affections.

They could have kept a camera crew hidden throughout campus to observe the mating rituals of these young adults and submitted the footage to *National Geographic* for scientific research.

Everything we did was an attempt to fan our feathers and garner the attention of a highly desirable—or at least suitable—partner.

I had my sights set on a girl a couple of years older than me. I was a sophomore, and she was a senior.[1] Not only that, but there were a few others interested in her, and they were seniors, too.

It became a battle for alpha supremacy, and eventually, I won. I wish I could say I took the victory with honor and grace, but truthfully I hoped their defeat would doom them each to a single and lonely existence. Call it a case of being a sore winner.

After months of dating, we were assured of our future together when we spoke the words …

I love you.

I can still remember the excitement when I saw her number on my phone or getting a text in the middle of the day. I remember how time felt like it was going in reverse while I sat in class waiting to see her. I had a hefty diet of caterpillars because I spent those early months with butterflies in my stomach.

We were *in* love.

It wasn't anything either of us necessarily chose; it felt like it just *happened.*

When we use this phrase, "in love," we are describing something many of us long for. It means being swept up in a current of joyful feelings and desirable emotions. It means losing control of our inhibitions and sensibilities and allowing ourselves to drift wherever our destiny takes us.

When you're *in* love, you almost feel like a victim. It's more like something that happens *to you,* outside of your control. Like you're someone selected without consent—held prisoner by affirmation and security.

Being *in* love is passive. It doesn't require much of you—just sit back, enjoy, and get married.

Which we did. And to our surprise, that initial feeling disappeared. As time went on, we came to a point we were no longer *in* love.

This happens in all marriages. You're riding the momentum of your excitement, but eventually, the relationship requires more of you. It becomes a choice you make. And it's not always the choice you want to make, which means it becomes work.

Ugh. Not exactly the thrilling blissful adventure you signed up for when you said, "I do."

This person who once made you the happiest you've ever been has the capability of making you the most hateful you've ever been, too.

That's not to say we didn't love each other. It was still there, deep down. But it started to feel more like love out of obligation—the way you say you love a family member you can't stand to be around or that slacker coworker on your otherwise reliable team. It's a sentiment, not something you feel.

Not something you're *in.*

We no longer experienced the condition or feeling we desired.

In the beginning, we were in love and had no intention to leave.

This happens when you're in a good circumstance. You scope out the terrain, investigate any possible threats, and settle into the exciting new world you've determined is secure. But somehow the environment changes. Your surroundings morph, and you suddenly find yourself somewhere else—*in* something else. You never packed your bags, but you woke up one day in a place you didn't expect—or want—to be.

At some point when you weren't paying attention, the tectonic plates shifted, the landscape changed, and the territory became unfamiliar.

What do you do when being *in* love turns into being *in* despair?

That was the problem in our marriage, and we had a clear answer …

Nothing.

When we fell in love, the feeling lifted us from the black-and-white farmhouse and dropped us into the colorful world of Oz. We weren't in Kansas anymore. We were walking the yellow brick road and enjoying every step. But Dorothy's life didn't just start in black and white.

It ended there, too. With the click of her heals, she mapped out a return home. She awoke from the dream, and—despite feeling a new sense of enlightenment—was back *in* Kansas. It's a sweet story, but am I the only one thinking life was better in color?

Is that how it works? Are some of us dropped into temporary prosperity trying to swallow it whole before we wake up to reality or before the next disaster takes it all away from us? Do we just get a glimpse of the good life, trying to hold on to the memories for when we inevitably return to the place we wanted to escape?

You have no control over the tornadoes that come spinning through your life. Sometimes all you can do is sit back and wait for the next one, crossing your fingers it will take you back to Oz or someplace like it.

So we did nothing and hoped it would work. We were growing increasingly miserable but didn't make any changes. We were both discontent and unhappy with our relationship, but we kept living the same way—repeating the same patterns.[2]

We simply waited for it to get better.

But the method of waiting betrayed us. So much time had passed that our marriage had been destroyed by the toxic habits and emotional dysfunction that had put it in such a dire state. Our relationship was unrecognizable from what it was when it all started. From the seed that gave it life. From the time we were …

In love.

And just like that, we went from being *in* something good to being *in* something bad.

Has this ever happened to you? Perhaps like us, it's your marriage? Or your job? Or a financial commitment? Or a friendship? Or a big life decision? Or a general season of life?

Have you ever stepped into something that gave you a sense of excitement, passion, or joy, and then the honeymoon phase ended, and it suddenly went south?

We're all *in* something, whether by choice or misfortune. It's your current circumstance. I don't know what you're in right now, so this section will merely allow you to self-examine your current state and diagnose its condition.

I hope you're in something life-giving and joyful, but regardless of what you've accomplished, or how happy you are at the moment, we all eventually find ourselves in a circumstance we desperately want to escape.

Facing what seemed to be my only option, I began preparing for the end of my marriage. It's not where we wanted to be all those years ago, but when the temperature drops, it's hard to resist the urge to migrate to a warmer climate.

Whatever it is you want to leave behind, we all have the same thought …

If this is the circumstance I'm in, maybe I can find a way out.

Letters in Exile

I used to love spending the night at my friends' houses.

Sleepovers meant junk food, relaxed rules, and later bedtimes. But regardless of how much fun I had with my friends, eventually, I'd want to be home.

Even for those of us who love traveling, there is a unique feeling associated with whatever we consider home—a sense of comfort, familiarity, and security. If you've ever spent significant time away from your home, you likely returned with a strong desire to reacquaint yourself with whatever seemed to be missing while you were gone. Family. Friends. Food.

And WiFi.

Your home is where you grew up. It's much more than a place cemented in the ground. It's a part of you. It helped shape you. Your home has meaning. It's a place you long to be.

Can you imagine if it was taken from you?

This is the biblical concept of exile. It's a time when the people of Israel were displaced from their homes after they were conquered by the Babylonian Empire. Some were killed, some were forced out, and some were allowed to stay.[3]

But for those that remained, life just wasn't the same. It was "home" … but not *home*.

This exile is an echo of another exile: when Adam and Eve were banished from the Garden of Eden. Despite the differences between these two examples, there is one common factor that unites them …

Being *in* exile is a place you're not supposed to be.

Whether you're exiled east of Eden or to Babylon, your surroundings are a reminder you're not home.

So what do you do? How do you get back? These are the questions Israel asked in Babylon. There were a few options.

They could fight.
But what happens if the remnant is killed? No victory is handed to a dead revolutionary.

They could flee.
But they can't reclaim their home running from it. And wherever they go could be worse than where they came from.

They could acclimate.
But how much would they be willing to compromise when their new way of life seemed to conflict with who they were and what they believed?

It didn't seem like there was a good option, and while the people were trying to figure out what to do, they nurtured stronger hatred toward Babylon.

And it's understandable. You would too. If you live in a place and a time without fear of Babylon kicking down the doors of your city gates, then you should consider yourself blessed.

But Babylon is more than an empire. It's more than a place on a map. It's more than an ancient group we read about in history books.

Babylon is a culture. A way of life. It's a representation of everything wrong in the world. When you find yourself in Babylon, you know you're in exile. And even though we might think of this as an ancient problem …

Babylon is alive today.

It's the place you're in that you want to escape. It's the circumstance making you yearn for a better life. You can hear the echoes of Babylon when you're belittled at work, abused in your marriage, attacked on social media, criticized by your neighbors, mocked for your dreams, and silenced by those with power and influence. It's the place that wants to tear you down, strip you of your identity, invalidate your calling, and make you conform to the culture around you.

It's a place where you just want to get …

Out.

When you're in a strange and uncomfortable place, it's easy to wonder if God is taking notice of your despair. It feels like he's gone quiet.

But he hasn't.

In fact, he's sending letters.

The prophet Jeremiah writes to the exiles in Babylon with these instructions from God:

Build homes. Plant gardens. Marry and have a family. Live a life that works toward the peace and prosperity of Babylon. Bless it, and you will draw blessing from it.[4]

Build a home in Babylon?

Did Jeremiah really just say that? Surely this letter wasn't proofread before it was sent. Passages like this must be why computer programmers created the squiggly red underline to notify us something is wrong in our document.

The people want out, and God is saying to settle … *in*.

Have you ever felt this? Have you ever politely requested—or maybe vehemently demanded— for God to remove you from a miserable circumstance, but the message you got in return was to stay put?

Before you jump to conclusions about your own situation, you should know this passage doesn't function as a universal guideline for every occasion. If you are being threatened or harmed, get out today!

But the truth is, sometimes our reaction is to run when God is really asking us to remain.

If that's a hard pill to swallow, then let's make it two. There is no easy return home from banishment. The road back is long and complicated, and it becomes longer the more you evade responsibility for your circumstances.

When you blame others and victimize yourself, you reinforce the reason for banishment.

It would be discouraging if this is where the letter ended. It would basically be saying, "You've made a mess; this is your new home; get used to it." But God says a bit more in the letter from Jeremiah.

"'For I know the plans I have for you,' says the Lord. '**They are plans for good and not for disaster, to give you a future and a hope.**'"[5]

When you're in exile, crying out to God, he is saying loud and clear …

I know this is hard, but I see you and I'm hurting with you. I understand why you're terrified—because this isn't how it was supposed to be. But don't run away and don't give up before I map out a new path for you. Just settle in for a bit—I still have great plans for you ahead. I will bring you home.

In some way, shape, or form, you're in—or will be in—exile.

And this is also God's letter to you—to give you a future and a hope. Relief is coming, but you might have to wait it out in Babylon longer than you'd like.

Offsuit Deuce-Seven

How did you get to where you are now?

I mean literally—in a physical sense. Where are you right now? In a coffee shop? Airport? Bedroom? Living room? The beach? Office?

Wherever it is, you didn't suddenly *appear* there.

You made a series of decisions that got you to where you are now. At one point, you stood up, moved one foot in front of the other, and whether you walked, drove, biked, or jet packed you arrived at the spot where you are now.

You can think back and trace your steps to understand how you got to your particular location.

And you can do this for more than where you are physically. Think about it in an emotional sense. Where are you? Are you happy? Sad? Anxious? Concerned? Afraid?

Think about it in terms of the circumstance you're in right now. Are you frustrated with your job? Are you in debt? Overweight? Struggling in relationships?

These things didn't just happen.

If you really think about it, you can trace your misfortune to where it started to materialize.

You don't always control what you're dealt. But you do control what you do with it.

Let's use the game of poker as an analogy.

In the game of Texas hold 'em each player is dealt two cards. The goal is to have the best five-card hand at the end of the round. If you're holding a pair of aces, then for the moment, you have the best hand at the table.

The worst hand you can be dealt to start a round is an offsuit 2 and 7—a deuce seven. This hand has the lowest statistical advantage.

In addition to the two cards each player is dealt, three communal cards are placed on the table for everyone to see.

This stage is called *the flop.*

Players then assess the quality of their hand. With their unique two cards hidden from the other players, combined with the communal cards available to everyone, a round of bets are made. Each bet signifies a player's confidence in their cards—or possibly their ability to bluff.

Another community card is made available. Now there are four cards on the table and two in each player's hand. This is called *the turn.* This new card changes the circumstance of the players. It might help or hurt their confidence.

A new round of betting ensues.

Finally, the last community card is placed on the table. This is called *the river.*

At this point, your hand is solidified. No more cards are available to change your circumstance.

At any point, a player can choose to fold his hand, meaning they are surrendering the round to the remaining players. Any bets previously made are given to the winner. But the game isn't necessarily determined by who has the best hand …

It's determined by who can make the most with what they've been given.

If you play the game long enough, become good at controlling your emotions, and take advantage of weaknesses in your opponent, then you can win the game **even if you're dealt a bad hand.**[6]

Even if that is unlikely, one thing is certain: you can never win a round that you fold.

The reality is sometimes in life you're dealt a bad hand. Something unexpected targeted you, and it brought disaster in your life.

These are things you simply can't control. A disease. The death of a loved one. Company-wide layoffs. Identify theft. Stock market crash. Stolen car. Natural disaster.

These are the situations where you are the victim. It wasn't your fault. It wasn't because you made bad choices. You lifted the cards tossed in your lap and realized you were holding an offsuit deuce-seven.

And so you folded.

That's a good strategy in poker, but it's not a great strategy in life.

Sometimes we keep folding—waiting for the right cards to come our way. We just patiently reject our circumstances and hold out for something more preferable. We check out of the game and spend some time watching other people play.

But even if you're successful at playing copycat, you will still be dealing with your own unique hand. You'll always have to adapt to the cards in *your* possession. And while you wait, you're losing chips. Soon you'll lose enough you can't play the game at all.

Here's the point: eventually—regardless of the hand you're dealt in life—you have to play the game. You have to make the best of what you've been given.

Sure, you can choose to blame the cards. You can blame the other players. You can blame the dealer. But it won't put you ahead. You need to learn what good poker players know, and it's this …

Some hands are bad statistically but not circumstantially.

Let's use the deuce-seven as an example. If you're holding an offsuit 2 and 7, then *statistically,* you have the worst hand in poker. That means it simply has the lowest odds of success before the other cards are laid out. So a player may prefer to fold.

Why invest when the odds are stacked against you, right?

But what if you chose to stay in the game? What if you decided to play out the hand you had been dealt? What if the flop, the turn, and the river produced 7-7-7-2-2?

Then you would have the absolute highest hand that round.[7]

That means the quality of your hand is relative to the outcome of your circumstance.

You really can't judge what is a good hand or a bad hand until you see how it plays out.

The problem, of course, is that we are too prone to fold before we can see the outcome. But who could blame you? Sometimes things are bleak with no indication it will improve. Why put yourself out there if there is a chance you'll be hurt or disappointed?

Let me say this, because it may be something you need to hear: You may have been dealt a bad hand. I'm not saying that to patronize you; I'm saying it to *validate* you. Your misfortune may have been slid to you from across the table, entirely outside of your control.

But you still need to take responsibility for what you do now.

Whatever you're contained, surrounded, or enclosed by—whatever you're in—you need to make the best of what you've been given. You can't spend your life folding and expect to reach a better tomorrow.

You have to play the game.

Silver in the Dirt

What if you decided to keep your life exactly how it is now? What if you mapped out the current trajectory your life is headed and somehow maintained course with flawless precision?

What if you kept all the same routines, habits, friendships, practices, and hobbies that are already cemented into your life? In 10 years, would you be satisfied or disappointed?

Essentially what I'm asking is are you currently aligning yourself to become the person you want to be?

Regardless of how you might feel about where you're currently headed in life, you're headed there all the same.

All of us have been able to identify something about ourselves we'd like to improve. Maybe you've made a New Year's resolution or set a particular goal for yourself that gave you a vision of personal growth or development.

That's good. It's something we should all do. But unfortunately, we know the tragic reality of making plans to improve but allowing time to pass without any movement. Why is it that these well-intended plans sometimes never materialize?

It's because a change was never made. You kept doing things the way you've always done them.

Your life is the perfect system to yield the results you're currently getting.[8] If you want different results, then the system has to change. If it doesn't, then things will stay exactly the same.

So, where is your life taking you?

Are you on the road to contentment? Will you look back and beam with pride in the ways you utilized your time, talents, and resources? Are you currently scheduled to reach your full potential? Are you now, or will you soon be, achieving a rich and satisfying life?

If not, then we are asking the wrong question. We shouldn't be asking where your life is taking you. We should be asking …

Where will *you* be taking your life?

You're in the driver's seat. You've been given the gift of free will, and that means you have a choice. And you are going to be held accountable for the choices you make, both in this world and in the world to come.

There are two ways you can approach life …

You can let reality dictate your dreams, or you can use your dreams to dictate reality.

In case someone hasn't told you, or you've struggled to believe it, I beg you to take this to heart …

There is so much more for you.

Maybe that sounds like a soundbite from a motivational podcast or a throwaway line from *High School Musical,* but it's true. It's been true since humans rebelled against God and found themselves east of Eden. It's what you feel in your soul when you look past *what is* to a picture of *what could be.*

You were made for more.

Your life is a resource, and you have been called to be resourceful.

Jesus outlines this concept with a parable in Matthew. He says it is like a man going on a journey who called his servants and entrusted to them his property. To one he gives five bags of silver, to another two bags of silver, and finally to another one bag of silver. Then he says that these have been distributed …

"… each according to his ability."[9]

That means each of these servants is accountable for how they manage what they have been given. Each has been given a resource and can demonstrate their resourcefulness.

When the man returns from his journey, he calls them to give an account of their investments. The one with five bags of silver produces five more and is praised for his resourcefulness. The man with two bags of silver produces two more and is commended for his resourcefulness. But the third servant serves as a warning to us all.

This is how he responds:

> *Master, I knew you were a harsh man, harvesting crops you didn't plant and gathering crops you didn't cultivate. I was afraid I would lose your money, so I hid it in the earth. Look, here is your money back.*[10]

Hold on, hold on … please tell me you caught it …

I was afraid … so I hid.

Why does this keep popping up? You start to get the sense the Bible is plagiarizing itself.

But that's because it is. Jesus isn't referring to a story. He's retelling *the* story. It's the story of you and me. So—in case it hasn't sunk in—once again …

Our insecurities cause us to hide from God and miss out on the life he has for us.

Clearly, this servant doesn't feel a sense of honor or gratitude at his assignment.

In other words, this servant tells the master, "I didn't do anything with what you gave me. I simply waited until this possession needed to be returned. Here; you can have it back."

Thanks, but no thanks.

And so he is cast out—banished. That might seem a bit harsh for a negligent financial return, but remember this is a parable. A parable is a teaching aid that Jesus uses to deliver a more profound truth. It's a story that reflects something happening within each of us. The resources and treasures God gives us are so much more important than an arbitrary bag of silver. Jesus confronts his audience with a severe illustration because we need to be aware that what we have been given is precious.

How else should God respond other than banishment when our bag of silver is a son or daughter, husband or wife, mother or father that we carelessly and lazily bury in the dirt? How else should God respond when we take the life we are given and use it to gratify ourselves, waiting to casually hand it back when we are done?

We are banished from the kingdom until we are willing to become the people God created us to be. Failure to be resourceful with what you have been given is a form of resentment against God. To be given the gift of your life and have nothing to show for it is like telling God your life was an inconvenience to you.

You are accountable for where you take your life and what you do with it. Jesus seems to believe you have the ability to make something of it. Something valuable and meaningful.

But it doesn't happen on accident. The list of goals we fail to complete is usually a bit longer than the successful ones, and that's because reaching our full potential requires us to be intentional.

Decide now where you will be taking your life.

A Better Tomorrow

Let's do a quick exercise.

Say you stumble upon a magic genie that grants you three wishes. What do you ask for?

No limits. Whatever you want, it's yours. If you're drawing a blank, here are some suggestions. Money, power, fame, possessions, new skills, more talent, physical fitness, a never-aging body, perfect immune system, more friends, travel, the abilities of Spiderman. You could even ask for the answers to some of the world's greatest mysteries like UFOs, the JFK assassination, or how much crack-cocaine Chick-fil-A uses in their recipe.[11]

For every person, there would be a unique set of wishes. No two people would likely want the same things. I couldn't possibly predict what you'd wish for, but I know something about you with absolute certainty …

You'd wish for … *something.*

No one is walking away from a genie saying, "No thanks, I'm good." Not even the people you think have it all. Why is that? The answer is simple …

Desire.

We all have desires. So let's frame our understanding of this term.

What is desire?

Easy. It's simply something you want or wish would happen.

Why?

Because it's something we imagine will improve our lives. It's something we imagine will satisfy us. Think about it as an equation.

You + what you desire = a rich and satisfying life.

Just fill in your three wishes with what you desire, and boom—your life is magically better.

Unfortunately, we don't have a genie granting our wishes, but we still strive to solve the equation. We're all trying to achieve a rich and satisfying life.

$A + B = C$ is easy to solve with numbers because we know their value. But our experiences have probably taught all of us that we don't quite know how to quantify the value of our desires. They can be deceptive and misleading. A rich and satisfying life is a pretty big solution, and a lot of our desires yield small or temporary gains.

So what do you want right now? What goal have you put before yourself? What's that thing ahead of you you're working toward? And before you get defensive, you should know desires aren't bad. It's good to work hard and strive to improve your life—whether it be the circumstances you're in or yourself as a person.

Whatever it is you're chasing—regardless of the stigma around it—it's at least a sign you believe a better future is possible.

That's the real point I'm trying to make. The way you live your life is a sign that you believe a better life—a better future—is possible.

And you know what? You're right.

A better future is possible.

Allow me to illustrate the proof of this theory.

What if I told you a better future *wasn't* possible for your life? What if I told you that every day from here on out, the rest of your life is only going to get worse until the day you die. You will never see or experience any joy or satisfaction ever again.

How would you respond?

I believe you would quickly reject that notion. Something inside of you would passionately protest in defiance of the dread and despair forecasted in your future.

What is that thing directing you to envision a better future for yourself?

Hope.

Hope that there is still truth and meaning and a better tomorrow ahead of us. That life is worth living. That wrongs can be made right.

We've all had some terrible days—some much worse than others. But when we lay our heads down, we are determined to believe that something better will come in the morning—or a morning to come.

Without hope, we are all just slowly inching our way toward the inevitable end of our days, void of the satisfaction we desire. We can hold on to hope, or we can let it disappear from our vision. That means we are all confronted with a simple choice: seize the time we have and live it for everything it's worth or sit back and watch our life dissolve until it's stripped of all meaning and purpose.

Life is only experienced when we choose hope. Otherwise, we're just walking toward our place in the grave. If you're having trouble deciding which path to take, it might be because you haven't learned why you're here.

It's time you found your purpose.

Either Way

When I was a kid, I hated school.

I hated sitting in class memorizing things I was sure I would never use.[12] I hated trying to come up with a meaningful contribution to the class discussion. And most of all, I hated …

Homework.

Seriously? We just spent 7 hours in this prison, and now you pile an extra 3 hours on my evening as well?

I'll be the first to admit: my struggle was my fault. I daydreamed, procrastinated, and never wrote down what my assignments were.

You know that feeling when the teacher says she's collecting homework, and you're frantically looking around the room thinking …

There was homework?

Yeah. That feeling of dread and regret in the pit of your stomach was a daily experience for me.

If you don't believe in God, you have to conclude all of life is just a random cosmic accident. There is no plan or design or intentionality. There is no purpose to life—it just *is.*

If this is your worldview, then here's the good news …

You live in a perpetual summer vacation, free of homework, midterms, or final exams. Your calendar is wide open, and you don't have anything on your schedule.

There are no assignments.

Nothing to turn in, and no one to turn it in to.

But …

If there is a God—if life isn't a random cosmic accident, if there is a plan and design governed by intentionality, if there is a purpose and you're given assignments—then you might one day find yourself frantically looking around the room thinking …

There was homework?

You are here for a reason. That means you've been given an assignment.

There is an interesting story in the Bible found in the book of Esther. This text is centered on a girl who is made queen of Persia after concealing her Jewish identity.

Through a series of events, the Persian king's right-hand man, Haman, develops a plan to oppress the Jewish people. He's going to convince the king to issue an irreversible decree for the destruction of the Jewish people on a specific date later in the future.

When Esther hears about this decree she is heartbroken and terrified. Her life would be in danger if her heritage were ever discovered, but she has the option to remain silent while her people are being targeted for genocide. After some time of prayer and fasting to discern what she should do, she visits with her cousin, Mordecai, and he says something profound.

"Who knows if perhaps you were made queen for just such a time as this?"[13]

Esther and Mordecai have a worldview that God can maneuver his people into positions of leadership and influence to address the challenges of difficult circumstances.

In other words, when you find yourself in a tough place, you need to know that you were made to face it head-on.

The Bible paints a picture of a God that brings order from chaos. He is intentional in action and moves with purpose. If that is true, then it is no accident that you are where you are. You've been chosen—you've been ordained—for this moment in time.

God is using the circumstances you're in to shape you. And if you're receptive to it, he wants you to shape those circumstances in return.

From God's perspective, chaos isn't happening to you—you are happening to chaos.

You're the agent that God uses to bring about change and renewal for the time and place you've been assigned.

People from Martin Luther to Martin Luther King Jr. have made historical impacts because they were aware of what needed to be done in their time, took responsibility, and led with the conviction that God placed them in their circumstances for a purpose.

But this is where we need to pause and make a crucial distinction.

Some people say things like, "Everything happens according to God's plan." But that isn't true.

God's plan was for all people to walk correctly in step with his perfect will. That plan didn't happen with Adam and Eve and it doesn't happen now. Every destructive decision we make is a glaring reminder that things most certainly do not go according to God's plan. His path for our lives develops according to the decisions we make.

God has a plan for your life, but you decide if you'll accept it or not.

This idea is presented earlier in the conversation between Mordecai and Esther.

He tells her, "If you keep quiet at a time like this, deliverance and relief for the Jews will arise *from some other place.*"[14]

That should humble you. Essentially what he is saying is that if you reject the responsibility God has given you—the plan he has for your life—then he will find someone else who will accept.

It means God doesn't need you.

If you wish, you can keep quiet. You can stand still. You can pass the opportunity to someone else.

Your life isn't scripted. Your story hasn't been written.

"Deliverance will arise from some other place," means it's possible to miss an opportunity that was offered—maybe even *intended*—for you.

The stage has been set; the characters are in place. But the part you play is determined by you. And if you sit back, then your opportunity may pass you by, and God will find another way—another person—to fulfill his purposes.

It doesn't mean he doesn't love you. It doesn't mean he's disappointed with you.

But it does mean you may be in danger of missing a gift he has for you. You may be in danger of denying an assignment he's selected for you. You may be in danger of sitting in fear while another rises in courage …

If you stay silent.

But you shouldn't. You should have the confidence to know …

You were made for such a time as this.

Don't get intimidated by your circumstances—own them. You might hear the voice of doubt asking, "Who are you to do anything about the mess you're in?"

But God is asking, "Who are you to do nothing about it?"

Have faith in God to do what only he can. But don't forget; he has faith in you to do your part, too.

No Pain, No Gain

Every moment of your life has been building to this one.

This very moment.

From the moment of your birth until now, you have been slowly moving to this exact place in time where you are holding this book, reading these words.

Every thought, every action, has formed you into the person you are now. And that person has been molded by challenges, victories, regrets, celebrations, doubts, risks, intentions, plans, and everything in between.

And all of these things have prepared you for what you'll face next— whether it be triumph or tragedy.

And from there, more moments will be added to the collection that makes up who you are. Each one contributing insight, perspective, and strategy to what you will face. This pattern will continue until you die. Or at least until you stop having new experiences—but hopefully until you die.

A great picture of this is the movie *Slumdog Millionaire.* If you haven't seen it, I apologize, but I am about to ruin it for you. It's a story of a simple young man named Jamal Malik who grew up in the slums of India and worked in a telemarketing company making coffee and tea runs for the higher-status employees.

Despite having no remarkable credentials or unique background, he becomes a contestant on an Indian version of the game show *Who Wants to Be a Millionaire?*

Producers of the show become suspicious when Jamal, a poor slumdog with no education, seems to know the answer to every question. Suspected of cheating, Jamal has to recall a story from his upbringing that explains his knowledge of each question he was asked.

He knew the answers because his life experience prepared him for the questions.

The movie draws on heavy themes of fate and destiny, but in another way, it's quite practical. Sure, your life experiences don't usually neatly align in a series of questions on a television show. That would force any of us to question if some cosmic destiny was at play. But in another way, isn't that just how your life works?

Your life experiences are preparing you for something.

We can even strip this idea to the nuts and bolts. It wouldn't take much searching to find someone successful in business to explain their journey toward achieving their dream was littered with failure, criticism, and discouragement.

And all of it prepared them for their big moment. It all paid off and equipped them to achieve their dream.

Athletes. Parents. CEOs. Entrepreneurs. Teachers. Doctors. Lawyers. Mechanics. Fashion designers. Dietitians. YouTube gamers. Inventors. Artists. Engineers. Factory workers. Authors.

All the challenges that came before the realization of their dream were the necessary obstacles that prepared them to achieve it.

Wouldn't it be great if every step we took was "up and to the right" of our growth projection? Unfortunately that's not how it works.

The successes are essential, but they don't prepare us half as much as the failures.

As the wise Jedi Master Yoda once said, "Pass on what you have learned. Strength. Mastery. But weakness, folly, failure also. Yes, failure most of all. The greatest teacher, failure is."[15]

Here's why I focus on this …

If what you're *in* right now is a season of failure, then you should be encouraged …

As long as you have perseverance. It doesn't help you to fail for the sake of failure. But if you're able to learn and adapt, then failure is the most significant catalyst toward success. Don't give up. If you are willing to allow one or two losses to keep you from crossing over to your vision of success, then you're not ready to grab it anyway.

If I were to ask you the three most defining moments in your life, what would they be?

Maybe some would be moments of great joy, but if you dig deep to trace the person you are now, you'd clearly see the moments of pain. When you were swept up in a sea of heartbreak, betrayal, grief, disappointment, and suffering, you were left with a scar. The things that you wouldn't wish on your worst enemy are the things that drastically determine—and maybe even define—the path you choose in life.

How have people managed to retain their resolve in dire circumstances? How have they found the strength to keep going when everything around them seemed to tell them to quit? How have some had the door slammed in their face and found the motivation to keep knocking? How have people overcome their failures to reach success eventually?

Paul puts it like this in Romans, "We rejoice in our sufferings, knowing that suffering produces endurance, and endurance produces character, and character produces hope."[16]

Rejoice in suffering?

That doesn't seem possible when you're in it. We've all heard the expression: *no pain, no gain.* It's a clever phrase when you're tying your shoes heading out to the gym, but it's a miserable reality when you finally step on the treadmill.

But here's the truth Paul is outlining: **pain is the only path to reaching our full potential.**

We all want the results, but not everyone is willing to put in the work. And the reason is so closely connected to our mentality.

Paul says that we can rejoice in our sufferings because he knows the end goal. He knows it is going somewhere. He knows it will guide us toward hope.

You can't rejoice in your suffering if all you can see is suffering.

Let's use an extremely basic example and put it in terms of your personal fitness goals. If you know the work you invest—especially when it gets painful—will eventually produce something that you desire, then you are willing to endure.

You can see that pain has a purpose.

It is shaping you. It is molding you. You need to prepare for pain because pain is what will prepare you.

When you pick up those weights or run a bit further than last time, it will hurt. And you will have to push through. You will have to endure. But your endurance will produce something. It won't just change what you look like; it will change who you are—a person that makes sacrifices and works toward a higher vision.

That's character.

But if you don't see the bigger picture—if you don't know what it is or don't believe that it is possible—then what will you do when you encounter pain?

Quit.

And why shouldn't you? No one wants to build endurance through unnecessary pain if it doesn't lead to something desirable.

That's why this other reminder from Paul has been so crucial to the Church for the past two thousand years:

"For I consider that the sufferings of this present time are *not worth comparing* with the glory that is to be revealed to us."[17]

This is about the bigger picture. If you trust that these painful experiences are preparing you for something greater beyond imagination, then you can rejoice in your suffering.

Like we've already established—no pain, no gain.

But again, easier said than done. We don't always see the bigger picture.

It's one thing to believe Paul was a wise man that inspired people with a vision of glory. But people can be misled, which is why they are misleading.

How can we trust Paul when he says God is working through our pain?

Great question. To answer it, we'll first need to ask …

Why Did the Chicken Cross the Sea?

There is a story in the Gospel of Mark that tells us after a long day of teaching, Jesus got in a boat and said to his disciples, "Let's go over to the other side."[18]

As they sailed across the sea, they found themselves caught in a horrific storm.

I guess Jesus wasn't much of a meteorologist. It would have been nice if someone had checked the local weather forecast.

We've all had at least mildly humbling run-ins with Mother Nature, but maybe you've survived some close encounters with tornados, earthquakes, tsunamis, lightning strikes, or hurricanes.

There is good reason to be terrified. You're helpless in elements outside of your control.

I've never been caught in a storm on a boat, but I've been a passenger on a plane flying through a pretty rough one through the night. It was a red-eye, and I was exhausted. But I was so scared I couldn't sleep. I've felt turbulence before, but several moments felt like we were being hurled out of orbit. At one point, all the lights went out, and I thought we'd lost power. I honestly believed the plane was going to crash.

We made it home safely, but I began to understand how the disciples may have felt in this story in Mark. Amid their chaos and panic, they are struggling to find something to grip. And then they look over to see Jesus is ...

Sleeping?

How can he be sleeping? Isn't he terrified? Can't he hear the wood cracking under the force of the waves?

So they wake him and confront him, "Teacher, don't you care if we drown?"[19]

Assuming their lives were over, I'm sure many things were running through the disciples' minds, like ...

I wish I was thirsty for saltwater because I'm about to inhale a gallon of it. Or, I really hope the story of Jonah was literal, and I've got an appointment with a big fish.

But along with whatever thoughts were in their heads, they were most certainly thinking this one ...

Why did we ever get in this boat?

When you find yourself in a storm, you begin to question all the decisions you made that brought you there. Hindsight is 20/20, so it's easy to craft a list of should-haves.

Maybe you're in a similar circumstance right now. Feeling helpless to the powerful forces that surround you, wondering why you did whatever you did to get yourself there.

When you look back, it's easy to think: *if only I had* _____.

The same is true of the disciples. *If only we had waited. If only we had said, "No." If only we knew what was coming.*

Why did we ever get in this boat?

But Jesus had already given a clear and straightforward answer to this question before they even set sail …

To get to the other side.

This line has been the punchline to hundreds of lousy chicken-road-crossing jokes, but it's also the word of God.

The storm makes us afraid, and fear makes us forget. We forget where we are going. We forget what God has said to us. We forget the calling he has placed on our lives. We forget what inspired us to take the first steps that led us to the storm to begin with.

In our fear, it's easy to think Jesus put us in the storm to die. He brought us here to drown in the abyss as we fade into the circumstances that are consuming us. He either doesn't care, isn't powerful enough to do anything, or he has forgotten us.

But that's not true.

Jesus is taking his followers to the other side. There is a destination in mind, and it isn't reached at the halfway mark. Jesus is taking them to set foot once again on dry land, but it won't come until they first get through the storm.

While the disciples are in a panic, Jesus is at peace.

So much so that he is sleeping. Not because he doesn't care, but because he isn't scared.

Right now, you might be in a horrible circumstance, caught in a storm in the middle of the night in the center of the ocean. And it's terrifying.

In these circumstances, it's easy to wonder, *where is Jesus?* Remember this story. He is in the boat. And he is taking you ... *to the other side.*

Do You Even Have a Choice?

Maybe you think you're ready to make a change. You're prepared to choose a new path—to choose hope. After all, you make thousands of decisions every single day—why not designate some of them to guide you out of a bad circumstance?

And what enables you to make a choice?

Free will.

You have agency over your decisions and are free to make choices for yourself. You choose how you spend your time, what to study in college, whom to marry—even important decisions, like what sports team to support or what new show to start watching on Netflix.

Of course, many of these decisions are conditioned by your environment. Your surroundings heavily influence the choices you make. But the fact remains that you are autonomous. You are not a programmed robot but an agent of free will. Right now, you can choose to continue reading or shut this book.[20]

... right?

Well, it depends on who you ask.

There are some who challenge the notion of free will for a variety of reasons. Some would say that you *don't* have free will. You can't make choices. That might sound crazy, but there are a few schools of thought that lead to this conclusion.

From a naturalist worldview, this belief is driven by your biology. You are simply the sum of atoms and molecules arranged and structured in a way that dictates your actions. The things you do are the result of neurological messages sent through your body to supply something it wants.

You are merely a walking bag of cells being sustained by chemical reactions in your brain.

You do what you do because biology says so. That would mean free will is an illusion.

Another view—one that doesn't exclude belief in God—is a theological view of determinism.

This perspective argues everything that happens is all a part of God's plan. You are a chess piece being moved by the divine on a cosmic board. You have no say—no control—over the path you take in life. You're saved or damned solely based on God's sovereign wisdom. The script has been written, and you're playing through the part you've been assigned. That's good news when you're cast as the prince but devastating when you're the pauper—or worse, you were handed the part of the shrub in the background. You simply stand still as you wait for the curtain to close.

You do what you do because God destined it to be.

But what if what you do isn't the result of biology or destiny? What if free will isn't an illusion, and the course of your life is determined by the choices you make? That would mean at best, these views are unhelpful. They only serve to mock your ambition and shackle you to your fate. At worst, these views are dangerous. They only help to release you from accountability and blindly justify all your actions.

Adherents to these views would defend them and I respectfully disagree. I think there is a much stronger biblical—and philosophical—case in favor of free will.[21]

You are not a prisoner of your circumstances. God enables you to choose another path. If you are unhappy with how things are in your life, you can make a *change* because you can make a *choice.*

This is good news for those of us that feel stuck in our undesirable circumstances. Again, maybe that describes the place you're in now. In that case, know this …

God is the author of your life, *but he passes you the pen.* You control the narrative. You write the story—for better or for worse.

Your future is determined by your faith, not your fate; free will is not an illusion.

If that's true then it's time to start taking …

Responsibility

The book of 1 Samuel is named after a prophet who leads the Israelite people and speaks to them on behalf of God. He is a gifted leader and directs God's people away from idols toward proper worship. God protects them from their enemies, and things seem to go well.

Until the people begin to compare themselves with their neighboring kingdoms.

They request that Samuel provide the people a king to govern Israel, just like all the other nations.[22]

This happens to us all the time. One moment we're content and the next, we're disappointed. And what is one of the driving forces behind this feeling?

Comparison.

Have you ever scrolled through social media and walked away feeling unhappy about your own life?[23] Instead of measuring our contentment against our own satisfaction, we try to align it with the people around us. When we see someone or something that appears to threaten our confidence—or even our intrinsic value—we form a desire to have what they have.

In the case of the Israelites, they want a king.

But the entire identity of this group of people was founded on their calling to demonstrate an *alternative* to the way of the other nations. They weren't supposed to do the things everyone else was doing. God was supposed to be their king. This request was a rejection.

If I were God, I'd undoubtedly be a little more than upset. Surely he will rain down fire and rebuke them in a voice of lightning for this, right?

But that isn't how the story goes. In fact, God does something extraordinary ...

He *grants* their request.

If that comes as a shock, then you need to know this—**God gives us the dignity of free will, even if we use it to reject him.** But it doesn't come without warning. God instructs Samuel to tell the people what life will be like when they follow the wrong king.

After a long list of undesirable outcomes, the people are relentless in their request.[24]

And then God tells Samuel to relay this message to the people ...

"When that day comes, you will beg for relief from this king you are demanding, *but then the LORD will not help you.*"

Geez. Leave it to God to hold a grudge.

I'd bet this verse never made it to any bumper stickers. I've certainly never seen it tattooed on someone's arm or printed on any motivational posters. It sounds a bit harsh—and highly discouraging. But ultimately, it echoes something we all should have learned from a young age …

We need to take responsibility for our mistakes. There aren't always convenient bailouts to the messes we make.[25]

We also learn something about God. He is willing to operate in sub-optimal conditions to accomplish a greater mission.

If you don't have room for this theological perspective, then you're going to have a hard time reconciling a lot of difficult things in the Bible. God accommodates our stubbornness, narrow perspectives, misguided worldviews, toxic habits, outdated traditions, and blatant ignorance to begin opening our eyes to a better way. Some may have different expectations for God. You may have heard (or had the thought yourself), "Why doesn't God just fix everything now?"

But that kind of thinking doesn't account for God's plan for your growth and personal development. It implies you're ready to inhabit a perfect, sinless world without first dealing with the root of sin in your own life.

We think the problem is that God's not ready to make the world right, but really…

We aren't.

And so we need some guidance. We need a leader.

Every kingdom needs a king, and this one is no different. The issue isn't the placement of authority or government.

It's the source.

We get mixed up serving the wrong king because we have our attention devoted to the wrong kingdom. The ideal is for the people to have the *same* head of leadership—to embrace God as king. We live in a world where people want things to be run like the other nations.

And so God allows it even though there's a better way.

It's a good time to pause and reflect on any times you've said, "Why is God doing this to me?" Now don't get too far ahead of me here. There are reasons and circumstances where that kind of question is a genuine and necessary approach to the problem of evil and suffering. I don't want to downplay or negate this crucial step in our spiritual journey.

But on the other side of the coin, we all know we point the finger at God when there are times we should be pointing the finger at ourselves.

Sometimes—and possibly even most times—we suffer the consequences of our own poor decisions. You can usually trace a difficult financial circumstance or broken relationship or lousy performance review to a poor decision you made long before it materialized into a disappointing outcome. We create the mess we find ourselves in, and have to take …

Responsibility.

We've already talked extensively about why that is difficult in "Part I." But taking ownership in a mess you're in means picking up a broom and getting to work.

Luckily God doesn't entirely abandon us to our own poor decisions. If the scales were weighed, they would unquestionably tilt toward God's grace, mercy, and intervention. The story of Jesus alone demonstrates that. Look at how this story of Israel and their request for a king continues. As Samuel transitions leadership over to the new king Saul, he says this to the people …

"Don't be afraid," Samuel reassures them. "You have certainly done wrong, but make sure now that you worship the LORD with all your heart, and don't turn your back on him."[26]

There is a critical line in this passage you can't afford to miss …

But make sure now ….

Even though they have dug themselves into a hole, God throws them a rope. They are given a second chance, and now a choice needs to be made. Climb out, or keep digging. Follow God, or follow someone else.

And in case it wasn't already obvious, Samuel finishes with yet another warning.

"If you continue to sin, you and your king will be swept away."[27]

There is room in the Bible for people to feel the weight of their mistakes. This isn't from a posture of vengeance or resentment on God's behalf. It's from a posture of mercy. God sometimes steps back so we can see how destructive our autonomy can be in our own lives. This is how God demonstrates that our way truly isn't better and that prosperity is found in obedience to him alone.

If you've made some bad decisions, and now you're feeling the impact of them, then this story serves to offer insight—but also hope. God has not abandoned you. He is with you in the self-inflicted pain, guiding you away from being like everyone else.

So you can become who you were made to be.

Count the Cost

If you want to make a change to the circumstances you're in, it's going to cost you something.

For most of us, the real problem isn't chasing our dreams; it's losing the comforts we have to attain them.

The simple truth is, you can't have it all. The road to your desired destination is paved with sacrifice, one way or another. You need to weigh the value of the assets you have against the things you want most. This needs to be done in all areas of life.

For example, you might feel stuck in a job you hate because it's providing for the lifestyle you desire. In this instance, you place more value on the life this job gives you than on the job itself. If you're satisfied, then this is fine, but if you're unhappy then you need to make a change.

And if you intend to make a change then you might need to sacrifice some of the comforts or luxuries you've grown accustomed to in order to pursue a career you might enjoy more.

But money isn't your only asset, and a career isn't the only thing you desire.

If you're unhappy with your health or weight, you'll need to change your diet and exercise routines.

If you're unhappy with your relationship with a friend or family member, you'll need to change the amount of time you invest in them.

If you're unhappy with your finances, you'll need to change your spending habits or your saving disciplines.

The change you're willing to make in your life always sounds good until you realize it means sacrificing something you value (or allows you to feel comfortable).

That's why so many of us decide it's easier to tolerate our undesirable circumstances than to sacrifice the few comforts we enjoy now. It's hard to step into the unknown when you at least have the security of what you have today.

This mentality makes you a prisoner. It means you're stuck in the circumstance you're in to protect the few benefits it provides. You're locked into a cell with no way out.

No one wants to be a prisoner, but there's something even worse …

A slave.

When you're a prisoner, you're *contained.* But when you're a slave, you're *controlled.*

Some of us are slaves, and we don't even know it. We're being controlled by our comforts, desires, expectations, and fears. We are controlled by the image we portray to the people around us or the status or position we hope to achieve.

These masters make us work for their elusive satisfaction. Freedom will come in the morning of a night that never ends. When you're a slave, all you can think about is freedom. To be released from under the thumb of oppression.

Or so it might seem …

When Moses led the Israelite slaves out of Egypt, it was a moment many didn't think was possible. After so many years of calling out to God for deliverance, they finally found themselves on the other side of the Red Sea.

And do you know what they saw?

Nothing.

There was no town. No homes. No beds. No food. No water. They were free to make a new life for themselves, but it meant starting over from scratch. They faced uncharted territory. For miles, all they could see was an open desert of sand and rock and hill.

This taught the Israelites that freedom comes at a cost. Freedom requires sacrifice.

Uncultivated land is fertile with possibility, but it is void of comfort.

Sometimes when you take a step toward the unknown, you begin to miss the certainty of what you left behind. You start to feel remorse about pursuing something new. Even though you've dreamed of this moment, you get a crazy thought in your head—a thought you *know* is crazy, but it creeps in nevertheless …

That life was *better* when you were a slave. That new life and freedom was a mistake.

In the case of the Israelites, as the reality of their freedom glares at them in the form of an empty desert, they begin to create fond memories of Egypt.

And so they complain to Moses.

> *Why did God bring us here? Has he forgotten us? At least when we were slaves, we had meat and all the bread we wanted!* [28]

It sounds a little unbelievable, but in this new, unfamiliar place across the Red Sea, they began to miss their old lives as slaves.

You and I know that it's foolish to sell your freedom for a few simple comforts …

We would never do that …

Right?

Hmm. It's enough to make you think.

This story doesn't just speak to the struggles of a small group of people in an ancient time of history. This story speaks to the struggle of the human condition. We all find ourselves trying to escape from freedom and return to Egypt. Sure, we may want to change our circumstances, but if it means sacrificing some of our comforts and walking out in an open desert, it might be easier to settle for the life we already have—even if it's subpar.

Here's the point: making a change in your circumstances will come at a cost. But before you cash in, know this: so will *not* making a change.

There is a cost to staying where you are, too. There is a cost to being a slave to the way of the world. If you are unwilling to make a change to your undesirable circumstances, it might cost you the life God has planned for you. It might cost you the purpose he has made you for.

Even the people closest to Jesus struggled to let go of the comforts of the life they had. To let go of their pursuit of status or power or influence. To let go of their vision of success.

Jesus asks them, "And what do you benefit if you gain the whole world but lose your own soul?"[29]

Running to freedom or hiding in slavery both require sacrifice.

The real question is which cost is greater?

Jesus makes it clear there is a correct answer. The cost of *not* following him is much greater than the cost of discipleship.

But that doesn't mean you march forward without recognizing what that cost will be. Until you know what the cost of changing your circumstances is, you likely won't even be able to move forward. The chains that prevent you from progress are the comforts you might be unwilling to let go of.

The promised land sounds glorious, but you'll have to sail on a sea of blood, sweat, and tears to get there. The truth is Egypt is *easier.*

But it's not better.

The life God has for you awaits your arrival, but it will require a change in the way you live, which means it will require a sacrifice of something you value.

You need to know the price of pursuing the life God has for you. Of creating a new circumstance. Of stepping into your true calling.

And Jesus warns, "Don't begin until you count the cost."[30]

Carry Your Cross

At the beginning of this section, I told you I found myself in a bad marriage. I had covered my insecurities with manipulation, emotional and verbal abuse, and selfishness for so many years that it was evident our marriage needed to end.

Which it did.

But we never got divorced. Instead, while I was driving one night to the place I had been staying while we were separated for a few weeks, God spoke clearly to me.

I didn't hear an audible voice or read a message conveniently placed on a billboard. It was something spoken in my heart …

Why do you think I embraced the cross? So I can walk next to you while you carry yours.[31]

Something in me needed to be put to death. My emotional dysfunction. My generational sin. My coverings I used to hide my insecurity.

My kingdom.

At that moment, I was naked before God. My shame was completely exposed, and I broke down.

But just like the disciples, Jesus got in the boat not to abandon me in the middle of the storm, but to take me to the other side.

It was a seed for new life. I went to counseling. I confessed my sin publicly. And most importantly, I asked God for a new heart. And over time, I changed. Don't take my word for it; ask my wife.[32]

Our old marriage ended—and it needed to—to make room for a new one.

When you experience—or should I say *encounter*—this kind of hope, it does something to you. It awakens something in you. It reveals something to you.

It peels back a layer unveiling an eternal mystery that allows you to get a vision of yourself and, ultimately, the world. It's a picture of your true potential. When you see it, you realize one thing …

It's not *your* vision.

It's …

PART III

GOD'S

|gäd| |GȮD|
Noun

1   (In Christianity and other monotheistic religions) the creator and ruler of the universe and source of all moral authority; the supreme being.

2   (God) (in certain other religions) a superhuman being or spirit worshiped as having power over nature or human fortunes; a deity, an image, idol, animal, or other object worshiped as divine or symbolizing a god. Used as a conventional personification of fate.

3   (God) an adored, admired, or influential person.

4   A thing accorded the supreme importance appropriate to a god.

I Had a Revelation

When I was about eight years old, I had a revelation.

It was in early December, and winter break was approaching at a painfully slow pace. But that built up the excitement and anticipation for the Christmas season. Snow was accumulating on the ground; it started getting dark outside before dinner, and the neighbor down the street had finally put up the last decoration piece of what became a tourist attraction, assembled with a small fortune and powered with enough electricity to get to the moon and back, twice. Our family was driving late one night, listening to Christmas music on whatever radio station started playing them before Thanksgiving, and I heard the same phrase repeated in almost every song ...

Merry Christmas. Merry Christmas. Merry Christmas.

Sung over and over, a phrase borrowed from one song to the next. Our car approached a stoplight, and I looked out my window to examine some of the decorations displayed over a small house. In bright red letters, it read the same phrase.

Merry Christmas.

As I studied the lettering, I noticed something that I hadn't before. I couldn't believe what I saw.

"Mom! Mom! Look!"

In a brief moment of panic, she gripped the wheel thinking we were in danger.

"What?" she said, tracing the direction my finger was pointing until she found the bright lights above the house.

In the silence, I realized she had not had the same revelation. She had missed the same thing I was missing all these years. But now my eyes were opened, and I would open hers, too.

"The word 'Christ' is hidden inside the word Christmas. Like the guy they talk about in church. Mom, do you see? Christ is the last name of Jesus. Jesus is a part of Christmas. And look. So is his mother, Merry. The Christians won Christmas!"

Mind-blowing, right?

I am embarrassed to say that this is a true story. And I was eight. Yeah. That idiot grew up and wrote this book you're now considering throwing in the fire.

But let me tell you why that moment was so memorable to me.

Growing up, it felt like God lived in the church. If you were good the whole week, you could arrive on Sunday and pray to him asking for things you wanted. If you were nice to your sister or did your homework, he might give you what you asked for. But at this moment, it seemed like God snuck out of the church and made his way on the rooftop of my neighbor's house. It felt like God was more active and present in the things I passed by every day—and yet never noticed him.

This was one of the earliest memories I have where I first considered that maybe God wasn't a part of *my* world …

Maybe I was a part of *his*.

Trust me, I recognize a story about a naive elementary kid discovering Christmas is about Jesus isn't fractionally significant enough to get you—or anyone—to believe there is a God out there. The only thing it proves is that the rituals, traditions, and foundational beliefs of Christianity have recognizably shaped our Western culture.

No one would argue that.

It's easy to look back and judge this revelation as unimpressive. Maybe you wouldn't even call it that. More like a reduction of ignorance. Today someone learned that $2 + 2 = 4$ or that the earth revolves around the sun or red and blue make purple. These are things you learn that don't feel particularly significant and won't likely change your life in any meaningful way.

But a revelation isn't just an accumulation of information; it's an encounter with *truth.*

It's being surprised by something that was there before you. It's getting a vantage point of something eternal; it preceded you, and it will outlast you.

That means any encounter with God is a revelation. It is an awakening to actual reality. And a revelation leaves a mark.

My story of coming to know God is what most would consider the typical journey. I was in 7th grade attending a Bible camp, and somewhere in between the free time at the lake on the blob and trying to find my soulmate, I had a life-changing encounter with the message of Jesus.

At that moment, while I was kneeling at the altar accepting Jesus as Lord, I sobbed like I was just sent home without a rose after hometown visits on *The Bachelor.* This part is gross, but I cried so hard I had to use my shirt as a tissue because the snot from my nose began dripping on the floor.

TMI? Maybe, but this is why I tell you all the gritty details. This revelation—that God has been real *this whole time,* and he loves me—made an emotional imprint on me. I didn't just *know* it … I *felt* it. It's a profound experience for those of us that can relate, but it creates an issue …

Sometimes we reduce God to a feeling.

The happy euphoria. The chemical shot of dopamine. The chills that run down your spine.

Don't get me wrong; those things aren't bad. God created your emotions, and he is working with them to reveal himself in your life. But emotions are unstable, and feelings change all the time. When we say things like "I just don't *feel* God's presence," it's because we're comparing it to a time we did—when we were in a different emotional state. We want *this* moment to feel like *that* one.

If you've been stuck in this cycle, here is something you'll need to accept to mature and move to the next stage of your spiritual development:

The truth of God is eternally constant, regardless of how you feel about it.

If you anchor your relationship with God on your feelings, you'll sway back and forth with every change in your emotions. How you feel is a terrible way to quantify God's presence. That's because your feelings can betray you.

That's why Jesus said to build your life on the foundation of doing what he said, not waiting until your feelings affirm it. Truth wouldn't be worth much if it had to wait for your permission to prove itself. Truth is already there—constant. And frankly, it doesn't care about your feelings.

But here's the bad news …

No one is guaranteed any kind of revelation. It isn't a matter of time. It's a matter of attention. God wants to be known, but there is a problem in receiving this revelation.

Concealment.

You are home in a world that is trying to conceal God from you. And the more God is concealed, the less we know about him. And the less we know about him, the more difficult it is to recognize him.

A revelation is bringing something to the surface, but concealment is burying it underground. A revelation is a discovery, but concealment is disregard. Revelation is an encounter; concealment is avoidance.

We need a revelation.

It starts with examining these human encounters with the divine, but that is only the beginning. In this section, we will work not only to understand who God is but also explore something he possesses—something that *belongs* to him.

Humans put a lot of thought into defining God, but the Bible is filled with stories where he is defining himself and defining us.

When we examine these stories we will learn they are moments where he is invading history to introduce himself and invite us to experience something new.

Luckily, God starts with where we are and challenges our misconceptions so he can reveal who he truly is.

What Do You Call That Place?

Do you ever wonder what your life would be like if you were born a few hundred years ago? It's hard to fathom how comfortable and convenient our lives have become because of modern inventions.

Your daily routine is filled with examples of human innovation and technology. Alarm clock, light switch, shower, coffee pot, refrigerator, microwave, laptop, television. And that's only what you use before you leave for work.

We've made quite a bit of progress in the past few hundred years.

At one point, every invention was revolutionary. Everything around you was born of a need and served a purpose of efficiency, convenience, or to reach beyond what was thought possible. But as our technologies evolved, eventually everything got replaced.

Not too long ago, someone said the phrase, "This walkman is the most incredible thing ever made!"

If you went back in time and showed that person Spotify, their head would probably explode.

How far back do you think you'd have to go in history to find someone that was genuinely impressed with the invention of … the brick?

At least as far back as Genesis 11.

> *"Come, let's make bricks and bake them thoroughly." They used brick instead of stone, and tar for mortar. Then they said, "Come, let us build ourselves a city, with a tower that reaches to the heavens, **so that we may make a name for ourselves**."[1]*

Early on in this ancient story, we see that society is advancing. They are accumulating knowledge and experience, which is shaping their technology. The brick was born of a need for efficiency, convenience, and to reach beyond what was thought possible. It may seem insignificant today, but this invention was a giant leap forward. When you have a brick, your walls are stronger, and your towers are higher.

And when your walls are stronger, and your towers are higher …

You can make a name for yourself.

In other words, people will notice you. People will talk about you. People will be impressed by you. People will respect you. If you build strong enough and high enough, people will even fear you.

And if you can invoke fear, then you will have power.

That's not just beneficial in terms of ancient kingdoms making walls and towers. We all want to make names for ourselves. We all want respect, love, and praise. Think about the ways you're trying to make a name for yourself now.

Climb the professional ladder. Get the corner office. Have over a million followers on social media. Make more money than you've ever dreamed of. Have the picture-perfect family.

Fill in the blank.

Making a name for ourselves is a constant pursuit for one thing.

Significance.

It's something we crave. We want to be praised, remembered, and celebrated. It's one of the ways we try to cover up our insecurities. We all want to do something worthy of our time here on earth. The world is home to billions of people who are each, in some way, shape, or form, trying to live a life of significance and meaning.

So what's wrong with that?

Well, if we track the biblical narrative, since the fall of Adam and Eve, the problems only increase. More violence. More destruction. More mess. More sin. But you don't have to rely on the Bible to see that reality play out. Just look at our world now to see what happens when people try to fill their need for validation or the ways they go to new extremes to stand out among the crowd.

Among the people that pursue honor, justice, and service are those that pursue vanity, oppression, and exploitation.

Our world is proof that when everyone is trying to make a name for themselves, there is no guarantee we will all be moving in a positive direction. In fact, according to the Bible, it's impossible.

So what do you do when you find yourself in a world where you're chasing all the wrong things and being told what you should do? How can you write a different story for your life? I guess the only thing you can do is "leave your country, your people, and your father's household."[2]

At least that's what God tells a man named Abraham. It's a pretty big request. So what's Abraham get out of it?

This is what God says:

> *I will make you into a great nation,*
> *and I will bless you;*
> **I will make your name great**...[3]

We live in a world of people trying to leave their mark and be remembered—trying to leave a legacy and find significance. Trying to accomplish something great.

This God comes along and tells Abraham, "You don't need to make a name for yourself. I will make your name great for you." That seems a bit too convenient …

Are you feeling skeptical? What's the catch?

Nothing big—just be a good dude, try to obey God …

Oh yeah, and take your son—your only son—whom you love, and sacrifice him as a burnt offering on a mountain.[4]

That's what God asks Abraham to do.

Dang. Should have read the fine print.

Pause. Does such a command mortify you? Do you wonder how God could ask Abraham to do such a despicable thing? Isn't God supposed to be loving? I mean, it's horrible; right?

Yes.

And thankfully, God agrees. In fact, that's the *point* of the story. Sometimes it's hard to read some parts of the Bible that describe God as loving when you suddenly stumble across other parts that seem contradictory. But your characterization of God has probably been formed through a much broader spectrum of Scripture, not to mention Jesus himself.

What if you knew absolutely nothing about God? Then you wouldn't have a framework of what you thought God may or may not do. You wouldn't have a framework of what you thought God may or may not say. And if you didn't have a framework, then, to you, there would be nothing outside of God's character. God could say or do *anything* and you'd simply accept it—even if it was something horrible.

Human sacrifice, as in Abraham's case, is an alarming request to you and me because we already have some concept of what God is like. If you casually told your family at Thanksgiving dinner that God was asking you to sacrifice your child, you would rightfully be met with severe opposition. They would tell you confidently that what you heard was *not* the voice of God; then hopefully call CPS.

You and I know that God wouldn't ask someone to do such a thing.

But Abraham doesn't.

Before you blame the poor guy, don't forget—this was the world he grew up in. A world where you sacrificed things you valued to get a few favors from the gods. The fact that he was headed up the mountain prepared to sacrifice his son seems to indicate that Abraham *didn't* find this request outside of God's character.

Apparently, God sometimes asks you to sacrifice your son. This would go against what God previously told him—that he would have a son and be the father of a great nation—so it looks like this God might break promises as well.

Abraham's view of God seems to leave space for corruption, manipulation, and lies.

I guess you could say that Abraham doesn't know this God very well.

Yet.

When Abraham and his son Isaac arrive at the top of the mountain, something happens. With his son bound by rope and his knife extended overhead, Abraham hears a voice calling out to him.

"'Do not lay a hand on the boy,' he said. 'Do not do anything to him.'"[5]

Wait … God doesn't want Abraham to sacrifice his son? Then why did he ask in the first place? Did he change his mind? Was this a test? Did God suddenly come to his senses? What is going on here?

Although this story shows us Abraham's faith, loyalty, and obedience to God, it's very important for another reason. This story invites a new understanding of who God is. **It is a story that subverts ancient expectations of what God is like and creates a paradigm shift.** This story is correcting misconceptions for an ancient group of people that have wandered very far from their relationship with the divine.[6]

What was surprising about this story thousands of years ago wasn't that God asked Abraham to sacrifice his son.

The surprising part was what came next.

"Abraham looked up and there in a thicket he saw a ram caught by its horns. He went over and took the ram and sacrificed it as a burnt offering instead of his son."[7]

God provides the sacrifice instead.

For God to do something like that, it would mean that he didn't want or need anything from Abraham. It would mean there were no strings attached in his offer to bless him. It would mean Abraham didn't have to earn God's favor.

What kind of a God is that?

Abraham is creeping into uncharted territory. There's no precedent for something like this. There's no spiritual category for a God that operates in this way. So here's the million-dollar question …

Why would an all-powerful God offer blessings and provide sacrifices for you?[8]

That's a question Abraham had to wrestle with. It's a question
we should wrestle with, too. The pursuit of that answer takes
us on a journey of exploration. The more you travel the path
toward understanding, the more you'll develop a sense of spiritual
wanderlust—the restless addiction of unveiling who this strange and
remarkable God is.

And so, among the many things Abraham does not yet know about
this God, he has just learned one thing: God doesn't ask you to
sacrifice your one and only son, whom you love. Instead … God
provides the sacrifice.

Something happened on this mountain—something powerful and
inspiring and life-changing.

Think back to the moments leading up to this revelation when
Abraham was fully prepared to demonstrate his trust and faith in God
in a way that would shatter his world. He was prepared to end the life
of his son. The days after God gave this instruction were surely filled
with fear and grief.

Then finally, the time had come, and Abraham was standing on the
mountain with his son, Issac.

What do you call a moment like that?

What do you call a place like that?

It's the place of your greatest fear. It's the place you are confronted
with the possibility of losing what matters most to you. It's the place
where you are filled with worry and anxiety. It's the place where the
future is uncertain, and the road ahead is unknown. It's the place
where you're sure you won't recover, and life will never be the same.
It's the place where everything is taken from you. It's the place where
life, as you know it, is over, and you're preparing to adjust to a
disappointing and heartbreaking new reality.

It's the place where all you have to offer is …

Faith.

But according to this story, it's also the place where God comes to the rescue. It's the place where you're surprised by his love and grace. It's the place you discover he doesn't need anything but wants to give you everything. It's a place where hope and joy replace fear and sorrow.

"So Abraham called that place *The LORD Will Provide.*"[9]

This is how many of us come to honestly know God. **In the places of our most desperate circumstances, deepest fears, or darkest secrets God shows up and provides what we need.**

It's the place God steps into your life and challenges everything you thought you knew about him by revealing who he truly is. The place where he changed your outlook from hopeless to hopeful. Where you traveled through mystery and awoke to a greater reality.

It's the place where God supplied you with a vision—his vision. It belongs to him. It's something that he generated. Something that he possesses. And it's something he offers as a gift.

You might not know everything there is to know about this God, but you do know that he is unlike what the world has been handing you. And now that you've had a taste you can't help but go back for more.

The world that always seems to take from you is contested by a God who wants to provide.

That's a good start if you don't know anything about God. But as we will see in the Bible, there's so much more.

So to take the next step, let's talk about …

A False Identity

It's important to know God because it's the only way we can truly know ourselves.

Abraham's son was Isaac, and when Isaac was grown, he became the father of twin sons—Esau and Jacob.

The name Jacob means "he grasps the heel," which was a Hebrew idiom for deceptive behavior. When Esau was born, Jacob clasped on to the foot of his older brother as if he was trying to pull him back into the womb, so he could be firstborn.[10]

Regardless if you're a younger sibling or not, we all understand this maneuver. There are moments we reach out in jealousy to those ahead of us and attempt to discretely pull them back so we can cut ahead. It stems from a feeling of scarcity. We are worried that by the time we reach the front of the line, what we've been waiting for might run out. Everything's already distributed—nothing left for us.

The day of Jacob and Esau's birth was the beginning of a sibling rivalry.

But Jacob didn't name himself. He was *given* this name by his parents. In this ancient culture, your name had significant ties to your identity. It was a reflection of what people saw as your potential. It was a representation of what your family thought of you.

So for Jacob, that meant being a deceiver. It's what his family thought of him, and therefore it's what they expected of him. When you're given an identity, there are two things you can do—oppose it or embrace it.

Expectations are a powerful force. It's much easier to swim with the current than against it. And that's what Jacob does. He lives his life as a deceiver.

And so, this becomes the backdrop for his relationship with his brother. When Esau returns from a hunt, starving and desperate for a meal, Jacob manipulates the circumstance for his own gain. He tricks Esau out of his birthright as the firstborn son for a bowl of soup.

Later, as Jacob's father, Issac, is nearing the end of his life, he takes advantage of another opportunity to exploit the situation for his gain. While Esau is out hunting to prepare a meal for his father Issac, Jacob intervenes during his brother's absence. He steals the blessing. At this point in his life, Issac is blind, so Jacob pretends to be his brother Esau by using the fur of a goat and wearing his brother's clothes.

And whose idea was this? Rebecca. Jacob—and Esau's—mother.

Wait … Jacob's mother encourages him to lie? That's pretty messed up, right?

But that's the identity she's given him. That's how she sees him, so that's what she expects of him.

But aren't his parents supposed to believe the best in him? Aren't they supposed to challenge him to reach to a higher standard?

Sure. But this isn't a new problem. You only need to look around—or maybe in your life—to see this reality play out.

Sometimes we are given false identities by the people that are closest to us. It could be a parent, a family member, a trusted coach or teacher, a close friend. These are people from whom we seek guidance. We ask them to speak into our lives and contribute to the vision of who we're meant to be.

To expand our vision of who we *can* be.

But in a broken world—with broken, insecure people—it comes out another way. Sometimes the voices don't echo what we can be. Sometimes they are stuck telling us what we *can't* be.

For Rebecca, it seems she doesn't imagine Jacob can be anything other than a deceiver. He can't be an honest man. He can't take a new path. And if someone you love and care about—that you think loves and cares about you—can't see your potential then you live up to their low expectations.

We permit ourselves to live into a false identity. And that's what Jacob does. But it isn't without consequence. When Esau discovers what Jacob had done, he begins making plans to kill him. So Jacob decides to run away.

At some point, we are all handed false identities. They are the unwanted souvenirs gathered in the territory of unrestrained insecurities. False identities trade hands like a regifted item passed from one person to another.

It's something we all have to deal with, but here's why it's so important …

False identities create a wall that severs you from reaching your true potential. God wants to help you break through it by embracing the identity he has given you.

This is God's plan. This is God's mission. This is God's vision. And those that are willing to courageously push to the other side are his people.

If you accept a false identity, it means you don't believe an alternative is possible. Maybe someone has told you that you're too dumb, fat, or ugly to have—or become—what you desire. Perhaps someone has told you that you're too irresponsible, incompetent, or incapable of reaching your goals. Maybe someone has told you that you don't have the talent, the vision, or the strength to chase the passions burning within you.

But if there are false identities, then that means there are … *true* identities.

So how do you discern which is which?

God Is Picking a Fight With You

As Jacob flees from his brother, he finds a place to rest. When he falls asleep, God comes to him in a dream and confirms the promise he made with Abraham and Issac. Jacob would be the father of a great nation that would be blessed and would bless the world. The dream ends with God telling Jacob that he would be with him and protect him. When Jacob awakes, he says, "Surely the LORD is in this place, *and I wasn't even aware of it!*"[11]

Jacob had heard stories of God. Stories where God made himself known to his grandfather, Abraham, and his father, Issac. He had grown up learning about God, but he hadn't experienced him the way his family had. He didn't have any divine encounters or spiritual epiphanies. He never felt the earth-shaking power, the humbling wisdom, or the heart-melting love of God that inspired those before him.

That's worth noting for all of us.

You can *hear* about God your entire life and never actually *know* him.

For Jacob, God felt distant—if even there at all.

That's why this dream was a defining moment for him. This encounter opened his eyes and expanded his awareness of God's presence. It's a presence that wasn't arriving just then—it had been there all along.

Sometimes we are waiting for our God moment. We want to experience the encounters described by other people where they were suddenly awoken to God's presence, and it changed their life. But what's important about this story is that Jacob claims encounters like these have always been available to him.

The problem isn't God's presence …

It's our *awareness.*

So what changes for Jacob to suddenly become aware of God's presence? Why would this revelation occur now and not sooner?

His awareness of God's presence enhances because he is running from the consequences of his actions. He's beginning to see that his way of life isn't working. Cheating people through deceptive manipulation creates enemies. Wherever Jacob went, he left behind a trail of broken relationships and angry people seeking revenge.

He finally realizes living a life embracing a false identity leaves you disappointed—desiring something else.

That's really how it works for all of us. When you're finally ready to admit your way isn't working, it's time to consider an alternative. And when you start to open yourself up to another way of living life … God is *already* there. He has been the whole time.

But this encounter with God isn't the end of Jacob's spiritual journey.

It's just the beginning.

Jacob finds himself in exile. And so it's time to return home.

But there's a problem. While Jacob was experiencing a radical change of heart, his brother, Esau, was sharpening his sword. Esau has been waiting, and Jacob's return home would finally give him the chance to quench his thirst for blood.

Jacob is paralyzed by the ensuing confrontation. He sends his family and possessions ahead of himself to soften Esau's resolve. But as Jacob gathers the courage to trail behind them, he encounters a man while he is by himself at the camp.

So what do you do when you're preparing to see your estranged brother that's been plotting to kill you, and suddenly you encounter a mysterious man in the dark at your camp when you're all alone?

You wrestle.

… For a long time.

… Through the night.

At least that's how the story goes.

In the heat of the match, Jacob discovers this is no ordinary man he's wrestling. With a simple touch, his opponent wrenches Jacob's hip out of the socket. His only hope is to cling to him and hold on for dear life.

As daybreak approaches, the man tells Jacob to let him go, but Jacob refuses unless he's given a blessing.

I'm no jujitsu expert, but I've watched enough UFC to know that some holds will subdue an opponent but won't give you the advantage of delivering any critical blows.

The match is a draw.

So this is how the man responds to Jacob …

> *"What is your name?" the man asked. He replied, "Jacob."*
> *"Your name will no longer be Jacob," the man told him.*
> *"From now on you will be called Israel because you have*
> *fought with God and with men and have won."*[12]

Hold on …

Was the man *God*? And Jacob *won*?

This is a bizarre story for sure, but don't let that distract you from the main point.

When Jacob was given his name at birth, he was also given an identity. Whether fortuitous or destined, Jacob lived up to his name. He became a deceiver.

He tricks Esau into giving him the rights of firstborn. He deceives his father, Issac, into giving him the family blessing.

But manipulation and trickery aren't the ways God distributes blessing. This mysterious man taught him that blessing would only be offered after an exhausting struggle with God through the night.

If Jacob's identity was rooted in his name, then a new name means a new identity. No longer will you be known for deception. From now on, you will be known for your struggle with God.

Once called Jacob, now called ... Israel.

This new name is interesting. The etymology of Israel is disputed. The story itself seems to indicate that this name means "struggle with God." Israel is the combination of two words in Hebrew—*Sarah,* which means to persist (translated as wrestle or struggle), and *el,* which means God.

Jacob struggled with God ...

And won.

So God can be *defeated?*

No.

Israel is also translated, "God persevorcs" or "God prevails."

To be clear, Israel can be translated two ways—"struggles with God (and won)," or "God prevails."

So which is it? Who is the loser in this fight? Here is the answer.

God and Jacob are both victorious—the match is a draw. The defeat is handed to another opponent.

The false identity.

To wrestle with God and win means to prevail over the false self. The self that is defined by conflict, lies, and deceit. The self that has been forged in the brokenness of sin and shame and insecurity.

God isn't defeated. Jacob is. Or should we say, Jacob was? Because Jacob no longer exists.

He is now simply contained in the memory of a new person with a new name—and a new identity. Israel is victorious because when he struggles with God, he discards the person he was and becomes the person he's meant to be. Israel wrestles with God to confront the lie of his past to create a new reality in his future.

A reality defined by his true identity.

This story makes one thing clear: **discerning your false identity from your true one will require a long and painful struggle with God.**

It requires tough questions. Why did you put me here? Why am I in this season? Why am I dealing with these circumstances? Why won't you bless me?

It requires sleepless nights. It requires leaving the comfort of the world you're in and stepping into the unknown world ahead.

It's only in the struggle that you find out who you truly are and who you're truly meant to be. But when you refuse to quit in your search for your true self—when you cling to God and refuse to let him go— you are given a new name and a new identity.

And what is the first thing Israel—formerly Jacob—*does* with his new identity?

He confesses to his brother and makes peace. He rebuilds a broken relationship. He takes responsibility for the pain he caused. He follows a new path.

This isn't something he could have done before this encounter with God. Jacob, "the deceiver," retreats. But Israel, "the one who struggles with God," restores.

In the Bible, names matter. And even though the names we are given today don't entirely correlate with the qualities and characteristics of our identity or personality, it's as accurate now as it was then ...

Names still matter.

And this God wants to write your name in the book of life.[13]

But it's not just our names that are significant, which is why Jacob asks this man to offer his name.

"Why do you want to know my name? The man replied. Then he blessed Jacob there."[14]

It seems like a copout. The story is over, and we don't get the name.

That's how the spiritual journey begins for all of us. We get a glimpse of the divine that pierces through the lens of our worldview, and it leaves us with more questions than answers. God arrives in unexpected ways, and we're left to make sense of it after.

Did God show up, or was that just a coincidence? Is there something out there, or was that just my imagination?

What was that?

Who was that?

A name is a way of establishing an identity. God knows our true identity, so he knows our name.

That means to know God, we need to learn his name.

Show Me Your Glorious Backside

I'm terrible with names. Even when I'm intentional, I still struggle.

One time I was at church with my wife, and we approached a woman we recognized from a previous event. She was with her husband, and it was his first time visiting. Trying to make him feel welcome, I reached out my hand and said, "Hi. My name is Matt."

"Pizza," he said, as we shook.

My mind froze for a moment. I understood he was giving me his name, but I knew I didn't hear him correctly.

"Sorry, what was it?" I said, asking for clarification. I zeroed in and gave my full attention.

"Pizza," he reinforced, with a smile.

I looked over to my wife, hoping she would recognize my dilemma and could find a way to bail me out. But she gave me the same look in return because we both heard the same name.

"Your name is … pizza?" I asked, as politely as possible, hoping that when he heard me say it, this man would realize the misunderstanding and correct me.

"Yes."

There was a moment of awkward silence. I didn't know how to recover.

I'm sure I embarrassed him. He'll probably never set foot in this church again. I wasn't trying to be rude. It's not his fault his parents were crazy. Who names their kid "Pizza?" Was his last name, Hut?

He broke the silence and began sharing how much he enjoyed living in the United States since leaving London a few years ago. As he spoke, the lightbulb came on, and it clicked.

Ohh … PETER! I finally realized. I looked back over to my wife, who clearly had the same revelation.

When he simply said his name, I didn't realize he had a British accent—*"Pee-tuh."* When he said it quickly, it sounded like he said pizza.[15]

If I had known who he was and where he was from, I would have had the context to understand him clearly. But because I had assumed he was American—and didn't anticipate his accent—I misinterpreted who he said he was.

Context is key. And when we don't have context, we fill the gaps with assumptions.

When I assumed this man spoke the way I spoke, I concluded his name was pizza.

The same is true of God. Because of how broken we are and how far we have wandered, when God tries to introduce himself to us, he can seem so foreign and unfamiliar that we don't understand who he actually is. Even when he tells us who he is, we end up hearing it wrong. And so, naturally, we fill the gaps with some assumptions.

We all have assumptions about God. Even people who don't believe in him have assumptions about the God other people believe in. Those assumptions might just be *why* they don't believe in him.

An assumption is accepting something without proof. That makes for a pretty big problem. How do we correct the false beliefs we have about God?

We need to ask for clarity.

There is an excellent example of this in Exodus. As Moses continues to develop a relationship with God, he says this.

"If it is true that you look favorably on me, **let me know your ways, so I may understand you more fully** and continue to enjoy your favor."[16]

Moses understands that there is a lot he doesn't understand. He's seen God at a glimpse, but he knows he needs more. And so he makes a big request.

"... show me your glorious presence."[17]

Up to this point, God has shown up in incredible ways. But Moses teaches us there is an important stage in our developing relationship with God. We need to seek him out. We need to ask him to show us his presence.

It is a request that is granted. God tells Moses that he will allow his goodness to pass before him, and this is how...

> Stand near me on this rock. As my glorious presence passes by, I will hide you in the crevice of the rock and cover you with my hand until I have passed by. Then I will remove my hand and let you see me from behind. But my face will not be seen.[18]

So. God has a hand? And a face? Does that mean when Moses sees him from behind, he's looking at God's ... butt?

In a way ... yes. But don't get too caught up in the physical descriptions. This story is assigning some anthropomorphic qualities to God to help us see what is important.

It's creating a picture of God with human attributes, so we can visualize what this experience is like for Moses. Does God really have a face? No. Not like you and me. But he does for this moment. And this is why it matters.

Moses doesn't get to see God's face.

*Why? Because it's too much to take in? Because he would
die on the spot?*

Yes. But that doesn't fully capture the poetry of this passage.

If Moses sees God's face then he would be in front of him, and you
can never get in front of God. He's always ahead of you, leading the
way. The only glimpse of God you can get is when you follow behind.
You can't see where he is going, but you can see where he's been.

**You can find him by following the trail of goodness
he leaves behind.**

But it's not just what Moses sees that enables him to know God more
fully. It's what he hears.

God says his name.

He identifies himself as *Yahweh.*

That name probably sounds a bit funny. Almost like you heard it
wrong. *"Sorry, what was it?"* So God repeats it.

Yahweh.

I don't think God has a British accent, but without some context, this
name will get lost in translation, and we won't truly know him. Who
is Yahweh, really? If we know what he's like, how he works, what he
expects then we can properly identify him.

Context is key, and here it is from God himself …

I am compassionate and merciful.
I am slow to anger.
I am filled with love.
I offer forgiveness.
I am the provider of truth, justice, and accountability—
they belong to me.

And I am working to correct the cycles of generational sin that you not only have inherited but threaten to pass down to future generations.[19]

This is what God says *Yahweh* means. We are able to understand who he is when we identify the qualities that define him. The trail that God leaves behind is flooded with footprints of compassion, mercy, patience, love, forgiveness, and justice.

It's the pathway to setting things right—in your life and your children's lives.

We all want restoration but don't always know where to find it. God is telling us to follow the trail he leaves behind. We can find it wherever we find the qualities he uses to define himself. That's why God shows us where he has been in our lives, and he is leading the way to take us where we need to be.

Your life with Yahweh means seeing him ahead of you with a vision of his glorious backside—trudging through the goodness his presence leaves behind.

I'm in the Mood for Some Wrath of God

As we continue to uncover who God is, we need to understand all the aspects of his character; even—or *especially*—the things that make us nervous, uncomfortable, or fearful.

The Bible makes one thing certain …

God hates sin. Like … a lot.

Maybe that's why you feel at odds with him. He hates sin—but you seem to love it—a major conflict of interest.

But God's feeling toward sin isn't merely an issue of preference. It's not like when you're battling over the remote control to determine what to watch when you find yourself defeated by an older sibling that's bigger and stronger.

God hates sin because he *loves* you.

Ahh, yes—there it is! God loves you. What a nice thought. It's inspired many older women to embroider loving Bible verses into fancy napkins or provide millennials captions for their Instagram pictures of pumpkin spice lattes or poolside shots in skimpy bikinis.

Maybe if God were seen as more loving, more people would be compelled to follow him. Many of us feel pressured to minimize all the stuff about sin and inflate all the things about love.

But if you want to know God, you can't avoid dealing with his posture toward sin. Eventually, you'll see another side of him that seems less appealing. One we don't want to experience. You don't have to read very far in the Bible to see that God's love is far too powerful to be complacent or passive or negligent.

God's hatred of sin generates a reaction, and that reaction is …

Wrath.

Wrath is a loaded word that comes with a lot of baggage. It's a term we use to convey intensity.

Wrath is a word we save for rare occasions. It's like the fancy dishes that only make their way out of the cabinet for special events. It's a word that means great anger and is reserved for dire instances.

The problem we have with wrath isn't the emotion. We all understand moments of intense anger.

The problem we have is the *target*.

Who—or what—is God's wrath aimed at?

You're fine with God's wrath as long as you're not in the crosshairs. No one has ever said, "Do you know what I'm in the mood for? Some wrath of God. I'd just love to experience God's anger and fury over my life's mistakes and failures."

But where should it go? You might not be aware of it, but you already have an answer to this question. There is a source of authority that determines where God's wrath is appropriately directed, and that source is …

Your pain.

Think about the things people have done to hurt you in the past. Think about the ways you've been mistreated, neglected, exploited, abused, disrespected, belittled, humiliated, cheated, deceived—the list goes on. Your pain is an atlas that attempts to direct God's wrath so you can receive what your pain truly desires …

Justice.

Justice is about making things right. **We crave God's wrath because we crave justice.**[20]

Someone—or something—has wronged you. It isn't fair; it isn't right, and something needs to be done. God's wrath brings us hope that our pain has been seen, validated, and it will be dealt with.

Justice matters. Without the promise of restorative justice for the sins committed against us, then all hope would be lost. When something hurts us, we demand that someone pay. Our world is full of brokenness, and there are a lot of wrongs that need to be made right. Too often, people get away with doing bad things.

Justice is about accountability. It's holding people responsible for their actions and dealing with the necessary consequences.

So, where do we start? Who should be the subject of God's wrath?

How about Hitler? He usually tops the list.

All parties responsible for 9/11? Definitely.

School shooters? For sure.

We've seen some pretty heinous crimes, and that's just in the past century. An exhaustive list would go on endlessly.

But that's just the people *all of us* might name. You've probably got your own personal list of people you think deserve God's wrath. People who brought you pain. People that should be punished—or at least harshly reprimanded. Regardless of whose name is on your list, they are all spelled the same …

J-U-S-T-I-C-E.

But God's wrath doesn't originate with a person; it starts with a problem.

The problem of sin. And it's a problem that affects us all.

We are grateful that God is working to make things right in the world when he's working to address *our* pain. But what happens when your name is on someone else's list? What happens when he's working to right the wrongs in someone's pain and the trail leads to you?

Wrath starts to seem like an excessive option.

But the wrath of God doesn't negate the love of God—it *enforces* it.

Whenever God responds with wrath, it's because he is administering his love. Sometimes we think of God like Bruce Banner and the Hulk. He has two different natures, and you hope to experience the pleasant side when the coin is flipped.

But God doesn't have two sides. He is constant; his wrath is an *expression* of his love.

And this expression stems from the destruction of his creation—his children made in his image—through the spread of sin and death.

The God of love is the God of wrath, and visa versa. The problem isn't *that* God gets angry …

It's *why.*

What God Isn't

Have you ever had something stolen from you?

When I was a kid, I never remembered to close the garage door when I got home from playing with friends late into the evening. Sometimes it would stay open through the night, and (more times than I can count) when morning came, I discovered something was missing.

I always dreamed of catching these thieves in the act. I envisioned them as hideous monsters, crawling out of the sewer, only to take delight in crushing the souls of the neighborhood children. I wanted to see their ugly faces and watch them run away in terror when I came out to confront them. That's what thieves do when they get caught stealing—they run away.

That was probably the most challenging part of waking up and discovering my red Huffy bike (complete with hand brakes and pegs on the back tire) was gone—I never saw it happen. I didn't know who stole from me. They were out there, somewhere, enjoying my stuff. And it all happened while I slept.

For as much as the Bible defines who and what God is, it also screams what he *isn't.*

God has a plan for you, and it's saturated in purpose. Jesus said his purpose is to offer a rich and satisfying life. That's an appealing offer, but God isn't the only one making plans for you …

While Jesus is mapping out the solution, he's also outlining the problem. Something stands between you and life to the full. He called it …

The thief. [21]

It's obvious he's talking about Satan, but rather than a name or a title, Jesus assigns him a description. He's trying to tell us something about the nature of this entity.

This enemy is trying to take something that rightfully belongs to God—and to you. He's trying to rob you when your guard is down.

A thief doesn't try to steal in the open, where he can be seen. His method is not direct confrontation; instead, he operates with discretion and stealth. He doesn't want you to be aware of what he is doing.

While God is working to make himself known, Satan is working to keep himself hidden.

That's what makes him truly dangerous. If you leave the garage door open, you might return to discover something valuable has gone missing.

So how do we guard ourselves against this enemy?

We need someone to watch over us. We need a protector. We need someone to shield us when we aren't aware of the enemies lurking around the corner.

According to Jesus, we need a shepherd.[22]

Someone to fend off the wolves that come to devour us.

Jesus refers to himself as *the good shepherd* who lays his life down for the sheep. But if there is a good shepherd then that means there is a bad shepherd. It's not just the thief or the wolves that keep us on our guard. Jesus tells us we also need to watch out for …

Hired hands.

They function as a shepherd for hire—guardians for rent. They'll watch after the sheep in exchange for a fee. That doesn't sound like a problem until Jesus gives this warning …

They will *abandon you* when trouble comes.

We have all shelled out our wallets a time or two for a hired hand. Someone—or something—we trust in to watch over us. Something to make us feel safe and secure. Maybe your hired hand is the plan you've mapped out for your life. You feel safe and secure when you feel like you're in control. Or maybe your hired hand is status—using your money, good looks, or position to get ahead. Perhaps your hired hand is your accomplishments. It's the trophies, accolades, or portfolios you've accumulated to feel superior.

These are the things we cling to that we think will keep us safe. The things that we believe will protect us from harm.

But Jesus warns us that none of these things are sufficient. None of these things can guard you against the true enemy—the one looking to rob you of the life you were created for.

When the real problems come, they will run and leave you to fend for yourself. A hired hand provides a false sense of security.

We surround ourselves with military, politics, science, medicine, information, weapons, degrees, relationships, goals, sex, money as a way to feel secure. But this is the critique Jesus offers each of these things …

They all fall short.

You may think you're using them, but they are using you.
They collect payment and leave you behind. They won't lay their life down for you.

We need something we can *trust.* Something that can take on the true enemy.

Is Jesus the Only Way?

A few years ago, I officiated a wedding and spoke to the mother of the groom at the rehearsal dinner. She steered the conversation toward my role as a pastor and simply asked how my journey brought me to this profession. After giving a summary of my path, she then asked about my views on the Bible, the Church, and the Christian faith in general. I detected a hint of skepticism, which was confirmed when she finally asked the question she had been waiting to ask all night …

How can Jesus be the only way to God?

This is a fair question and one that we all should be asking.

How do you reconcile the idea of a loving God offering salvation through such a narrow channel? How many people throughout history have lived and died and never heard the name, Jesus? Is there good news for them, or have they been forgotten? What do you make of the millions of people that go on a genuine search for God and end up in another religion? Were they bad at finding him? If you find Jesus, is it because you're more blessed or just simply superior in some way?

Who doesn't want to be on the other side of the table to questions like these in a room full of family members to the couple you're about to unify in marriage 24 hours later?

In order to frame my response, I needed some context. So I asked …

"Are you opposed to Jesus?"

"No, not at all."

"But you wouldn't call yourself a believer?"

She thought about it a moment before finally labeling herself.

"I guess I'd say I'm … spiritual."

What this mom articulated has become the appealing label of many people in our current cultural moment. For most people that label themselves as "spiritual," it means they acknowledge that something is at work in the universe (something unseen and mysterious), and this something provides us with meaning and purpose.

Someone spiritual feels a common unity among people of different faiths and backgrounds and worldviews and disregards any dogmatic differences because, in the end, we can't really know what God is like. We can just hope to assemble a useable framework of the divine from our experiences and allow it to develop over time through the unique path we choose to take in life.

No one is right—everyone is right. You do you. Follow your compass.

That sounds enlightened until you're lost in the desert and discover your compass doesn't point north.

At some point in life, we all need direction. We all need a reliable metric of right and wrong. We all need truth, and the truth is only valuable if it doesn't *agree* with everyone.

On one level, I admire the humility of claiming to be spiritual. I think such a person rightly acknowledges we can't fully know or comprehend God. Claiming to be spiritual allows space and freedom for God to work outside of the parameters of our expectations.

But what it misses is a sense of authority.

Without a reliable source, how do we know our desires don't manufacture our spirituality? How do we know it's God that's forming us and not us forming God? How do we know our spirituality isn't a display of our craftsmanship in the process of carving an idol in the shape of our aspirations?

Acknowledging a universal spirituality is one step in the journey, but it isn't the final step. We're still miles from our destination—if our destination is to know God.

People have always been drawn to spirituality. While many outspoken atheists argue our world is simply material, the rest of us are convinced there is something more. This isn't anything new. Human beings have always been searching for God.

But this is the good news of Jesus—**that God has always been searching for you.**

That's why we need to talk about Cornelius.

We are introduced to Cornelius in the book of Acts. By today's standards, he was a "spiritual" man. Everyone in his time was spiritual. The question wasn't *if,* but *which* god you served, and there were many to choose from. Cornelius was a Roman centurion. That means, according to the Jews, he was considered a gentile. This caused a fair share of tension in the culture because it was no secret the Jews had contempt for the gentiles. They wouldn't associate with them because they thought it would make them impure. The nature of the Jewish laws, traditions, and practices conveyed a message of religious and moral superiority over everyone on the outside.

If you weren't a Jew, you didn't know God. If you wanted to know God, become a Jew. Pretty simple.

Now a Christian might be quick to criticize this kind of posture. I mean, how can God be so exclusive? Isn't that why we have Jesus? You have to follow him because he made a way for *all* people.

In other words …

If you aren't a Christian, you don't know God. If you want to know God, become a Christian. Pretty simple.

Hmm. Seems like the same narrative with a different proper noun. So, back to Cornelius.

As a Roman centurion, Cornelius was a man of position and power. We don't have a lot of background on him, but his story comes after the death, resurrection, and ascension of Jesus and the start of the early Church. The Bible gives him this description.

"He was a devout, God-fearing man, as was everyone in his household. He gave generously to the poor and prayed regularly to God."[23]

The Bible seems to think pretty highly of a man that wasn't Jewish or a follower of Jesus. Let that sink in for a moment.

So one day, when Cornelius is praying, he has a vision and is told to send some men to retrieve Peter, a disciple of Jesus. And so he does. When Peter arrives, he is told why he was summoned and then proceeds to offer this message …

> I see very clearly that God shows no favoritism. In every nation, he accepts those who fear him and do what is right. This is the message of Good News for the people of Israel—that there is peace with God through Jesus Christ, who is Lord of all.[24]

The story of Cornelius tells us from a biblical perspective that you can have a real relationship with God without knowing Jesus.

Mark a tally for the "I'm spiritual" group.

But here's the whole point of this story—his relationship with God is *incomplete.*

For Cornelius to grow and mature in his relationship with God, he needs to know Jesus. If he doesn't send for Peter, he simply remains a God-fearing man who gives generously to the poor and prays regularly to God.

You might think that doesn't sound too bad. Isn't that good enough?

But his vision tells us something different. Apparently—according to God—being a God-fearing man who gives generously to the poor and praying regularly to God *isn't the goal.*

Having a spiritual encounter is one step on a path that awakens you to the reality that there is more to life than what you simply see, hear, or touch.

And if you continue to follow that path, it will take you to know Jesus—which is another way of saying, know God.

Being a spiritual person can only take you so far. Eventually, it will become the very thing *preventing* you from knowing God. Like any real relationship, we need more than general ideas, vague descriptions, or shallow concepts.

This story in Acts tells us that if we want to know God, then we need to encounter the good news of Jesus.

Taste

Sometimes I struggle to believe that Jesus is enough. That he will wholly satisfy me in a way nothing else could. A good reason for that is hunger.

Let me explain what I mean.

When you don't eat, your body responds with a reaction. This reaction is designed to get your attention so you can provide it with something it craves. A hunger pang is your body's way of screaming, "Feed me!" You can't misinterpret this reaction. That tightening in your stomach sends a clear message. Your brain will also jump in. You'll start thinking of some of your favorite foods and begin mentally scrolling through your mealtime Rolodex until you've identified which craving is speaking the loudest.

You put food in your mouth. The hunger goes away.

… for a little while.

But then it returns, and you go through the cycle again.

And again. And again.

And over time, you give a little more authority to that hunger. Maybe you move a bit quicker to meet its demands. Perhaps you grant a little more governing power to your cravings. And those cravings have begun to evolve to a specific taste. The stuff that's blanketed in cheese or coated in sugar usually has the most sway. Then one day—to your surprise—you step on the scale and realize the number has increased.

So you resolve to lose some weight by starting to eat healthier meals. Looking at the calendar, you circle the upcoming Monday—because everyone knows a diet can only start on a Monday—and binge in the days leading up to it as a goodbye ceremony.

Monday comes, and you're feeling motivated. Your healthy breakfast—or skipped breakfast—is your first step toward reaching your goals. Some of you might breeze through the early few days; for others, the struggle begins an hour after your normal fueling time.

But one way or another, your cravings and your hunger are going to catch on to your little plan.

And they will protest.

Aggressively.

The rest is up to your will power. Do you have the perseverance to reach your vision and the self-control to reject the temptations that want to sabotage your goals? Some of it depends on which cravings you've nurtured and for how long.

Let's put it this way—getting one hundred dollars out of debt is never fun, but it's a lot easier than climbing out of a million.

Your consistent decisions empower your habits, and sometimes they grow so strong they commandeer your thought process and start making choices for you. Sometimes your cravings grow so strong it seems like they've already won. It's easier to give in at this point.

When that happens, it's no longer a craving …

It's an addiction.

Let me ask this—if every food *tasted* like your favorite food, what would you eat?

Let's say option #1 in front of you is your favorite dessert, and option #2 is a bowl full of veggies that tasted *exactly* like your favorite dessert.

Which would you choose?

Obviously, the healthy option. If both options *tasted* exactly the same, then it would be foolish to reject the one that also has nutritional health benefits.

That's the problem. Most of the time, the things that taste the best aren't good for you. That's true of more than just the foods you eat. It's true about most things in life. So brace yourself, because this might not settle well …

Jesus doesn't *taste* better than sin.

Before you give this book a zero-star review on Amazon, let me explain why …

If this weren't true, everyone would be a disciple—whether they believed in God or not.

This shouldn't come as a surprise. Taste is an *immediate sensation* to something you consume. The immediate sensation to all sin is delight. That's what makes it so tempting. Who doesn't want a quick shot of euphoria?

Every single temptation you face is a promise of immediate bliss.

But let's go back to the taste metaphor and reduce it to what it truly is: a brief moment of pleasure. When something tastes good, it is a pleasurable experience. But if we simply let our taste dictate our decisions, we will experience disastrous consequences.

Pleasure is a poor metric for the desirable life. If you don't believe me, just look at a heroin addict. They seem to experience a high level of pleasure with unrestrained intensity all the time. But we don't elevate these individuals as something to be celebrated in our society. Few people would say a heroin addict has discovered the formula for the good life.

I've never done heroin, but I'm sure it's wonderful.

Why else would people be willing to throw away their money, jobs, homes, family, or friends just to get their next fix? Their brief high seems to be purely euphoric, so why don't we all have a drug dealer on speed dial?

This is why ...

Because even though taste matters, there are many more meaningful ways to measure satisfaction. Your body isn't the only thing that gets hungry.

Your *soul* is hungry, too.

But how do you feed a soul?

Jesus makes it clear to his disciples. He says, "I am the bread of life. Whoever comes to me will never be hungry again. Whoever believes in me will never be thirsty." [25]

When we consume Jesus, we will be fully satisfied in all the ways that truly matter. He is the sustenance that supplies what we need. But it doesn't mean your cravings for other things go away. As you try to detox, they will only get stronger. Which means you'll need to make a choice.

Will you feed your flesh and starve your soul or feed your soul and starve your flesh?

There isn't enough to satisfy both hungers. And a choice to save the one is also a choice to destroy the other.

What's Behind Door Number Two?

As we continue to let God define himself in our lives through the stories of the Bible, we need to address the fiery elephant in the room …

Hell.

I think one of the most common critiques of Christianity comes down to the idea of God's sentencing of a non-believer's eternal destination. You've heard these arguments at some point in your life.

"Why would a loving God send people to hell? How come God doesn't just save everyone?"

There are many layers to these questions, and how someone responds is often merely a reflection of their doctrine or theological persuasion. But regardless of what you believe about heaven or hell, there is a common gap these questions fail to recognize …

We have an affection for sin, and the places it's available masquerade as a paradise.

So imagine this:

You've just died and are now standing in a room with two doors. One door is open, and Jesus is standing in the doorway. The other door is closed.

Which door do you choose for all eternity?

The choice might seem obvious at first. You choose Jesus, right? Even if you didn't believe in him on earth, you stand to reason at this moment you were wrong. But hey, if he'll let you in the door, then this is great news. Free pass! Live however you want during your life and still make it into heaven? Who knew it could be so good. I guess everyone does get saved in the end.

You would take the Jesus door to heaven because door number two is obviously "the other place," and who would choose that?

But you'd want to take a peek, right?

The curiosity of your potential damnation is just too much to pass up. You'd want to see how bad it would have been if Jesus wasn't in such a forgiving mood. Maybe you imagine turning the knob of door number two to find a bunch of demons dancing around a fire, blasting Nickleback on repeat, feeding you mountains of kale.

You'd slam the door shut as tears poured from your eyes in an overwhelming reaction of gratitude that you were headed somewhere better.

Okay—maybe we shouldn't joke about hell.

The truth is, I'm sure you imagine taking a peek into a truly dreadful, hopeless place you wouldn't wish on your worst enemy. You probably could imagine the paralyzing fear that would come from simply gripping the door handle. Like when you're standing on top of a cliff and feel tempted to walk to the edge so you can see how far the bottom is.

Your legs start shaking. You move slowly and cautiously. Then the second you satisfy your curiosity, you shuffle back to safety while the tickle in your groin dissolves.

Here's a confession … I'm terrified of door number two but not for reasons you'd think.

I'm afraid what lies behind door number two isn't a lake of fire or an army of fallen angels with sharp teeth and red horns.

What I'm most afraid of is nervously checking to see what's behind door number two and discovering …

An *empty throne.*

I'm afraid what lies behind door number two is a kingdom of my making. It's full of the promise to deliver whatever my heart desires. It's full of money and power and sex and fame. It's full of songs of worship that celebrate my glory. It's full of everything I've ever wanted and the promise of so much more. It isn't engulfed in flames, but rather it's packed full of servants, ready at my beck and call. I'm their king. Door number two contains a lonely crown and a clear path to seize it.

If I stood there staring at both open doors, is it possible I could mistake which one is heaven and which one is hell?

So many of us spend most of our lives choosing door number two here on earth. Does it seem reasonable we'd choose door number one after we die? There are different views on hell,[26] but what I want to challenge you to consider is that it might be a place that subverts your current expectations.

That is what makes it so scary.

Jesus says he has prepared a place for us in his kingdom, **but it's a place where *he* sits on the throne.**

There are no governmental vacancies. There are no empty chairs in the judgment seat. He rules supreme, and life with Jesus means life *his way.* The way we see in Scripture that he modeled here on earth. Jesus says door number two is a place of destruction. Where there is weeping and gnashing of teeth. Sure, that's a horrific picture, but my concern is that I'm so blinded by sin that I fail to see how destructive it truly is.

It *appeals* to me.

What if hell doesn't look how I imagine it? What if suffering looks like something I crave? What if the separation from God truly is what I desire? What if my perception is so skewed by my sin I can no longer recognize the goodness of Jesus?

What if he is absolutely everything I need, but nothing that I want?

Jesus says door number two is hell. And some days, I can't turn the handle fast enough.

The Divine Invitation

But divine judgment and a person's eternal destination aren't the only critiques we have for the character of God. There are other qualities God reveals to us that describe who he is that create challenges for us.

If Jesus was who he said he was, then that means he possessed *absolute power.*

Sound's nice, right?

But it presents a difficult question: If Jesus had the power, why not use it to get what he wanted?

Isn't that what power is for? The ability to manipulate and maneuver people or events through the use of force to get your desired outcome? Why didn't Jesus just slip on the infinity gauntlet and give a Thanos snap to the world and make everything as it should be?

It's a fair question and one that the Bible answers. But another important question we must all ask ourselves—a question that reveals something about who *we* truly are—is …

If *you* had ultimate power, what would you do with it?

Most of us would have the same kind of answers.

Do good. Put an end to suffering. Fix problems. Make the world better.

So what's the delay? If we could see how easy that is, why can't God?

Well, let's ask another question …

What do you do when you have ultimate power *but face resistance?*

What do you do when you're trying to do good, put an end to suffering, fix problems, make the world better, but some people oppose those things?

Do you destroy them? Do you lock them away?

This is the question presented to Jesus at the foot of the cross. The people mocked and ridiculed him saying, "He saved others; *let him save himself* if he is God's Messiah, the Chosen One."[27]

According to the people present at the crucifixion of Jesus, he should have exercised his divine power to rip the nails from his hands and feet, jump to the ground unwounded, and flex his muscles in a show of strength. He should have used his power to save himself.

Why do the people say this? Because that's what *they* would have done.

And why would they have done this? Because they had a different agenda than Jesus.

The kind of power we expect to see is a demonstration of strength that can be used to create fear and intimidation. This kind of power can be used to force the people into submission.

That's how the world exercises power.

Those that have it use it to impose their will on others. Jesus said to his disciples, "You know that the rulers in this world lord [their power] over their people and officials flaunt their authority over those under them."[28]

That's what we're used to. It's the narrative of random, unintentional evolution—survival of the fittest. If you have the power, you're entitled to have what you desire.

But Jesus critiques this use of power. He tells his followers to take another approach.

But among you, it will be *different* …[29]

Instead of saving himself and making them suffer, Jesus suffers at their hands to save them. Jesus doesn't dismantle the cross and strike his enemies down. He embraces the cross to raise his enemies up.

Because when you raise your enemies up in love and life, they aren't your enemies. They become your friends. And when you turn enemies to friends …

You win.

But the battle still rages. Your ego is in the way of turning an enemy into a friend, and fighting a person you think is your enemy is a much easier opponent than your ego.

That's why Jesus commanded his followers to use their power in a different way. Instead of a show of strength, they were to offer a show of service.

Jesus didn't use his power to destroy the people who rebelled against him because he believed there was hope for them to change.

It is that very show of love and service that makes way for a change. No one has ever been the target of hate and changed for the better. It molds them in a way that they become guarded, defensive, and hostile to protect themselves.

In other words, they become insecure.

When you hurl arrows at your enemy, they will justifiably put their guard up. But when you serve them in love, they can let their guard down.

Truthfully, as someone who follows Jesus, I will admit I find it hard to align my beliefs with the vision Jesus has for lost people.

If I'm honest, there are some people I just consider … *hopeless.*

There is no way for them to change. There is no possibility for them to turn from their destructive way of life. Too much time has passed. It's too late for them.

This is a true confession because it is a sin I need to repent from. And as far a sin goes, this one might be the worst. You've probably heard (or said), "All sin is the same in God's eyes." It's true that we have all fallen short of the glory of God, but not all of our sins have the same consequences here on earth.

Considering some people hopeless has the most devastating consequence of all.

If I consider someone hopeless, I can justify withholding my love and service from them. I mean, why waste it, right? But if I manage to justify a reason to withhold my love and service, how will they ever encounter the vision of the kingdom or experience the love that God has entrusted to his people to spread throughout the nations? How can they experience transformation if we imprison them to their current condition?

And what do you call it when you create the reality you predict?

Self-fulfilling prophecy.

When you determine someone is hopeless and treat them as if they are hopeless, you have created the reality you have predicted.

Prophecy is a gift of God because it is an indicator of the work God is doing to restore. A self-fulfilling prophecy is a curse because it is an indicator of the work we are doing to destroy.

Your plan is not better than God's plan. Until you accept that, you are living as …

A false prophet.

Hopelessness is an abuse of power. It's how I lord my authority over the people around me. It's how I control and determine who is worthy and who is a lost cause.

It's how I destroy them. I guess I *can* answer the question of what I'd do if I had ultimate power.

It's a question I answer every day by the people I choose to serve and the ones I label hopeless.

That's what makes the power of Jesus so intriguing. He maintains hope that people can change because of his vision for them to be saved.

That is salvation according to Jesus: rebellious, sinful people turning from their hostility and being transformed by his love.

Jesus—and his followers—use their power to serve others as a means to reveal a different kind of kingdom than the one we see every day. A different kind of people than the ones that surround us. A different kind of king that rules with love and justice. And a different kind of destiny than the one set before those of us who have fallen far from the ways of God.

How does Jesus exercise his power?

Invitation.

When people are intrigued to know more about Jesus and the life he is offering, his response is …

Come and see.[30]

There is no threat. No show of power through force or manipulation.

It's an invitation.

And an invitation to all. Because according to Jesus,
none are hopeless.

If you struggle like me to believe Jesus on this, it needs
to be repeated.

All are invited. None are hopeless.
All are invited. None are hopeless.
All are invited. None are hopeless.

Burn it into your heart. Carve it into your mind. This belief fuels the
way Jesus uses his power, and in turn, commands the use of power
for his followers. When you consider people hopeless, you deny them
the invitation Jesus has given you.

You're invited to invite.

And why are you given this liberty? Because all people belong to God.
We are his possession. Remember, this section is not only about
defining God but defining us. When we know who God is then we are
able to discover who we are and whose we are.

But if that invitation doesn't interest you, then you don't have to follow.
You can choose to accept or reject.

Jesus won't force you into his kingdom. He has hope you will freely
choose the invitation.

No One Else Is Coming

We all have—or have had at one point—hope.

It fuels our outlook on life and enables us to become more than we are today. We may not all hope for the same things, but at some level, every single person on earth has desires they wish would materialize and become a reality. This is true of more than just the things you want for your life.

You have hope beyond yourself. You have hope for others. You have hope for the community of the world. You have hope that a better tomorrow awaits us all.

But every society is full of individuals asking this question …

Who—or what—will get us there?

What belief, practice, system, or person will *deliver us* to the promised land? The land flowing with milk and honey. A place of prosperity and peace.

The human pursuit of utopia is unceasing. We all crave a perfect world inhabited by a perfect life. But by what means will it arrive? How will we get to our destination?

Do your accomplishments drive your hope? Can you achieve your dreams simply by applying the proper work ethic? Does luck drive it? Are you hoping the stars will align, and you'll scratch that winning lottery ticket? Is it driven by faith? Do you believe there is something out there giving assurance that a better world is on the horizon?

These are the questions everyone is asking, and the way we live our life is a reflection of how we answer them.

The human race is universally united on *what* we want: a perfect world.

But we are very much divided on *how* we will achieve it. Where should we invest our hope for this desire? By what means will it arrive? These questions have ended many conversations in hostility, tension, offense, and hatred.

This is why we have wars. This is why we have different forms of government. This is why we build walls and collect nuclear weapons. This is why people argue on Facebook. This is why you hate Fox News or MSNBC or whatever mouthpiece articulates the opposition of your political party. This is why Mormons come to your door or why people shout into megaphones on crowded street corners. This is why people gather to march in protest through the streets of the city. This is why we have an education and encourage our children to do well in school.

It's because we are passionate about the hope we have for a better world, and we *advocate* for the pathway we believe will take us there.

All of these things are what different people perceive as the means to a brighter future. Each one of these approaches is connected to a person that believes they have a solution to the problems we face and seek to conquer any and all opposition.

All these investments of time, money, and energy are collective deposits of humanity working toward prosperity—either for themselves, their people, or the entire world.

Every significant person remembered throughout history worked toward their vision of a better world. Gandhi. Hitler. Malcolm X. Stalin. Rosa Parks. Lincoln. Anne Frank. Obama. Pharaoh. Moses. Caesar. Jesus.

They put systems in place. Or ideologies. Or practices. They mapped out paths to their desired destinations. They offered visions and dreams of something better.

But who among those we remember—or among those to come—can *deliver* on their promise?

I guess it depends on who you ask. Were you the beneficiary in their proposals, or did they perpetuate a change that cost you something? Did their hopeful vision of a better future require undesirable change on your part?

To an Israelite slave, Moses was a liberator, but to Pharaoh, he was a thief.

Who wins when your vision of a better tomorrow comes at great cost to the status quo? There is always someone greatly benefitting from how things are, and people benefitting will generally fight to *keep* benefiting.

With so many competing visions of a hopeful future, some will win, and others will lose. When there are opposing desires, eventually someone is going to have to either compromise or worse: abandon their vision altogether in defeat.

The same goes for you. There are forces opposing the direction you're headed in life, regardless of what direction that is.

The point is this: we live in a world with endless conflicting figureheads, proposals, and ideologies that promise to deliver a better tomorrow. They can't all be right.

Whatever—or whomever—you choose will take an important role in your life. It's the role of ...

Messiah.

Your selection will become your savior—to usher you and others into the promised land.

That's why we put bumper stickers on the back of our cars during elections. It's a way of communicating with the people around us ...

This is our deliverer.

But it's not just politics. We find all kinds of ways to advertise a clear solution to the issues that surround us.

Sign up for this membership. Attend this seminar. Donate to this cause. Watch this video. Share this post.

And each one is a subtle nudge to believe that if only _____, *then* things will be better.

I don't know how you'd fill in the blank, but I know how the Bible would.

"I, yes I, am the LORD, **and there is no other Savior.**"[31]

Yahweh, the savior, outlines a plan for a leader—a messiah—the one who can deliver us. And if you're waiting for something else, you'll be waiting until you step foot in the grave. The Bible makes it clear—**no one else is coming.**

A better world will not arrive when your candidate is president or when technology advances or when medicine develops or when science provides us with new insight.

All of those things might be good, but they are not the promised messiah. They fall sort of delivering what we truly need: healing from the disease of sin.

God doesn't just provide a diagnosis but a treatment. He wants to heal our brokenness and eliminate the sin that is consuming us like a cancer. God is awakening us to his presence. He is trying to capture our attention when we are unaware of his movement. But when we catch a glimpse of God—when we see his goodness leaving behind a trail for us to follow—we know this path isn't ours; it's his. It belongs to him.

And this path of healing is God's plan for making you ...

PART IV

HOLY

|*ho·ly*| |hou-li|
Adjective

1 Dedicated or consecrated to God or a religious purpose; sacred: the Holy Bible.
(of a person) devoted to the service of God: *saints and holy men*.
morally and spiritually excellent: *I do not lead a holy life*.

2 Used in exclamations of surprise or dismay: *holy smokes*!

Judging a Book by Its Cover

If you Google "what is the best selling book?" you'll get a number of links that direct you to a list of popular titles. Even highly successful books in recognizable series like *Harry Potter* or *The Lord of the Rings* pale in comparison to the sales of *A Tale of Two Cities* — which, despite its impressive figures — is still lagging significantly behind *Don Quixote.*

These lists of book titles — and many like them — are members of an elite club of literary works. They are praised for their widespread popularity and continue to leave store shelves year after year.

But what's interesting about these lists of best-selling book titles is what they are all missing ...

The best selling book.

The Bible is excluded from these lists, but not because it can't contend with the leaders. It's not only the best selling book of all time ... it's also the best selling book of the year, *every year.*

If that delights you for whatever reason, you should be hesitant to celebrate. The Bible is excluded from these lists because it has somewhat of an unfair advantage. Studies show that over 90% of homes in America have a Bible, and the average total number of Bibles in any given household is four.[1] I don't know about you, but most people aren't buying multiple copies of *The Da Vinci Code* or *The Alchemist.*[2]

And as impressive as it is that such a large number of Bibles are produced and sold, the reality is that most of them go unread. For many people, the Bible in their home functions as a quiet sentiment, a relic to honor tradition, or a cautious superstition.

The word Bible comes from the Greek word *biblos*, which simply means ... are you ready for it?

Book.

When you're reading the Bible, you're reading "the book." It's not much of a title, but more of a reference. It describes the collective works that have made their way through time and territory to be assembled into one unified story.

Before the Bible was assembled, it was a group of scrolls that contained the teachings, history, stories, and writings of the Jewish people. After Jesus, the stories of his life and the letters to the early Church were added by his followers into a complete collection many of us recognize as the Christian Bible today.

At this point in history, the term Bible is recognizable. If you told someone that's what you were reading, they would know exactly what you were talking about.

We are all very familiar with this book, but do you know what's written on the cover? I'll give you a hint … it's not "The Bible." If you don't believe me, grab one of your one-to-four copies and check.

It's easy to miss, but an adjective is assigned to this ancient library of religious texts. What's written on the cover is …

Holy Bible.[3]

It might seem like an insignificant detail, but it's how we can judge this book by its cover. You aren't just reading any book. You're reading a *holy book*.

The cover gives you insight into the nature of its contents.

But the reason you may have missed this detail is that no one ever says they are reading the "Holy Bible." That just sounds … weird. It's a word we don't use or reference in everyday life. The Bible might be the only place you even see the word "holy." It's not something we throw out in casual conversation. You'll likely never eavesdrop on office gossip where the criticism is someone's holiness …

"I just hate working with Frank. He's not very holy."

"Does this salad have bacon in it? I'm watching my holiness."

"We've seen some significant improvements to Jessica's work performance ever since she got holy."

These aren't things anyone says.[4] We don't include holiness in our day to day conversations. It feels like there isn't much room for it in our vocabulary outside of a religious setting. Besides, does it even matter?

The simple answer is yes. It actually matters most. But why it matters is what we will explore in this section.

We will need to look in the only place that seems to have a use for this word …

The book.

Oh, sorry; that wasn't specific enough.

The Bible.

Songs of Deliverance

What comes to mind when you think of the word holy? It's not a trick question. The common answer for most of us is probably God.

Yes, God is holy. The Bible says so …

Eventually. But it doesn't happen right away.

The first time you'll find the word holy in the Bible is early in Genesis, but it's not in reference to God. It's in reference to the seventh day of creation.

"And God blessed the seventh day and declared it holy because it was the day when he rested from all his work of creation."[5]

The word holy comes from the Hebrew word *kadash,* and it merely means "to be set apart." In that context, there is no shortage of things you could deem holy. If this was our only understanding of the term then you could say the quarterback on a football team is holy, your private bedroom in the house is holy, or your only blue crayon in the Crayola box is holy.

These things are set apart from the rest—distinguishable.

We know there is more to it than that because our understanding of this term is shaped by more than this one reference. But it will require some patience because this is the only time the word holy is used in Genesis. We don't come across another reference until the book of Exodus.

In the form of a burning bush, God appears to Moses and instructs him to remove his sandals because the ground on which he is standing is holy.[6] It seems pretty clear in this passage that wherever God is present, the area surrounding him is somehow affected.

That's certainly interesting, but still a little indirect. Not quite the reference that forms our understanding of this term.

The next time the word is used is in reference to a festival.[7] Hmm. That's not enough either …

A day. A small square of land. A festival. We're more than a few pages deep into the Bible, and so far, this is all we know of what it means to be *holy.*

For a word you'd instinctively associate with God, the Bible certainly seems to have missed this important connection. If you're reading cover to cover, you will have read 64 chapters before God is even directly called holy. It almost seems to diminish what we thought we knew of this term. Maybe this word isn't as special as we thought …

But that all changes when we get to an essential part of Israel's story.

From Adam to Moses, we are invited to observe a God that is deeply invested in his people. Despite failures and compromises on their part, God responds with favor and promises of blessing.

But the journey isn't without brokenness. From the time it takes you to turn the last page of Genesis to the first page of Exodus, the people of God have gone from prosperous to prisoners.

They have become enslaved by Egypt and cry out to God for liberation.

And their cry is heard. God gives Pharaoh several opportunities to turn from his oppressive rule and free the people he has captured. When he doesn't, God takes over. He parts the Red Sea, which enables his people to cross safely to the other side[8] and begin a new life.

What's the first thing these people do in this new reality of freedom?

They sing. And what's their song about?

God's *holiness.*

> *Who is like you among the gods*
> *O, LORD—*
> **Glorious in holiness,**
> *Awesome in splendor*
> *Performing great wonders?*[9]

This is the first time God is directly called holy in the Bible. And what is it in reference to?

Freedom.

The liberation of the people.

A song of deliverance from a place—and a state—of captivity.

These newly freed slaves claim that God is holy. And this is no arbitrary descriptor to separate him from other gods in this ancient culture. It's not merely an adjective to inflate his identity.

They sing about how God's holiness does something.

God's holiness translates into rescue and renewal. God's holiness brings deliverance from slavery, oppression, and tyranny to a new life of freedom.

According to the Bible, it is *because* God is holy that his people are freed from their slavery. There is something about who he is that fundamentally opposes the powers that enslave his people. This quality of God is the catalyst for liberation. Meaning this …

God's holiness not only brings freedom—his holiness defines what it means to be free.

Sometimes we think freedom is doing whatever we want, but that way of thinking is a trap.

When you march out into the world with no boundaries, compass, trail, or guide, it appears like you possess unrestrained, unlimited freedom. But if you're unfamiliar with the territory and haven't learned to be cautious, it won't be long before you wander into a bear cave, fall in a snake pit, or rest in a lion den. The boundless freedom you were enjoying might feel like a curse when you stumble upon something that starts tearing into your flesh.

Absolute freedom enables you to choose something destructive, addictive, constrictive, and limiting. And when you're trapped in these patterns, you feel anything but free.

Real freedom is not doing whatever you want. Real freedom is found within the boundaries that protect you from being controlled by your disordered desires. And this boundary is defined by holiness.

If that is true, then we need to become very familiar with this word. We need to understand what God's holiness has done for the people in the Bible. We need to understand what God's holiness can do for us. God later reminds his people of this historic moment. He says, "I am the LORD, who brought you up out of Egypt to be your God; therefore *be holy because I am holy.*"[10]

Be holy?

That feels like a tall order. I don't know about you, but I picture a boring life as a monk, spending my days praying with my hands clasped like I was giving myself a high-five, maintaining a reverent expression, and singing notes that sound like drawn out yawns. It's not a very appealing command.

But here's the good news: that's not what God is asking.

Living a holy life is about living the life you were made to live. When you are holy, you are most yourself. You are your true self. And if you are your true self, then you are living your best life. Another way to look at this verse might be ...

Live life to its full potential because I made you to live your best life.[11]

That's a different spin on it. And it's certainly a lot more appealing than some of our false presumptions.

This command is about aligning ourselves with the qualities of God because those qualities function as a map to take us where we truly belong—a place of freedom.

Holiness is about deliverance. It's about being rescued. It's about being set free.

For now, let's begin with this perspective: holiness is right living. The best kind of living. The kind you were made for.

So the question we must ask is—how do we become holy?

Tell Us the Truth

You are going to die.

Hopefully, not today. But someday. And you want to know something else? I don't even have to know you to say this about you. This statement isn't rooted in any particular quality you possess. It has nothing to do with who you are, where you've been, or the choices you've made. I don't have to interview every person in the world to verify the certainty of this claim.

It is simply …

True.

And for it to be true, it has to hold up regardless of the variables surrounding it. For it to be true, it can't be dependent on certain conditions. It would have to be absolute. It would have to be universal.

And if death is inevitable, then so is pain and suffering. Either your surroundings or time will do violence to your body. Your heart will stop, and your flesh will decompose.

We all will die. We all feel pain. We all experience suffering.

These are universal truths. They are experiences known to every human being. There is no religion, worldview, or ideology that excludes this reality.

In fact, most systems of belief are created based on how to deal with these truths.

I'm sure in the height of your suffering, you have probably had this thought:

Things are not as they should be.

Maybe you'd phrase it differently …

It isn't right. It isn't fair. Why me?

Regardless of the language you would use, it comes from a narrative you've crafted of what the world, or at least what the human experience, should and shouldn't be.

So what do we make of this? Our pain and suffering experiences continue to trample over us, regardless of our efforts to avoid them. So we must craft an explanation.

How have you already reconciled this problem in your worldview?

Is the Devil, or worse—God—the one engineering the evil and suffering you experience? Is it karma from the wrongdoings you've contributed to the world? Are you, or people in general, to blame for all misfortune? Is it the simple reality of an indifferent universe that neither knows or cares about your fragile existence?

These options are oversimplified, but one way or another, you'll have to decide one of them. This is very important and can't possibly be overstated:

How you live your life reflects how you reconcile the reality of pain, suffering, and death.

So today is test day. And there is only one question:

1. Why do we suffer and die? *Circle one:*

       A. A divine mystery concerning God, the Devil, and human sin.

       B. What goes around comes around, until you reach nirvana.

       C. People make bad decisions, and one way or another—for one reason or another—they pay.

       D. You are cells temporarily manifested in consciousness—your existence is mathematical and it will be over soon because you are slowly decomposing.

If you haven't studied, maybe you can take a guess.

Ennie, meanie, miney, mo.

That strategy has worked before. And even if it doesn't, who cares? As we all said in high school, *"Are we really going to use this stuff in the real world anyway?"*

Maybe we file it away with geometry or algebra. The formulas we learn to get the grade we need to graduate and never think about it again.

But whether you know it or not, how you answer this question determines the way you live your life. It determines the way you make decisions. It determines the hope you have for your future. It determines your priorities. It determines your character.

If everything isn't as it should be, what can we trace as the source of the problem? And just as importantly, what can we trace as the source of the solution?

Let me use an example. Let's say life is a cosmic anomaly of infinitely small chance and circumstance that has produced the universe and everything in it. So make a selection …

[Circles D]

We suffer and die because we are conscious organisms caught in the indifferent continuous development of nature governed by the laws of an unconscious universe. The world was formed in a violent explosion of heat and energy. You don't matter and you won't be remembered.

Geez. That sounds pretty grim. But don't look so down. This can be good news. If you choose this answer, you've just selected the gospel of secularism! If this is the correct answer, then think about how you get to live your life …

Do whatever you want. Be whoever you want. Live your life while you can before your time is up. Eat, drink, and be merry!

I'm not saying this sarcastically—I mean it.

If there is no God or karma and suffering is the result of an indifferent universe, you should spend every waking moment chasing whatever makes you happiest the longest. Keep in mind you still live under the tyranny of society and have to play by the rules of the game. If you don't weigh the consequences of your actions, your joy might be short-lived. You could end up in prison or lose all your money, so you'll want to make some calculations.

Here's a basic formula to get you started: maximum happiness and minimal cost for the longest time possible. Master that, and you, my friend, have found the key to the best life.

But what if you circled D, and got it … wrong? What if your answer wasn't *true?*

Then the way you choose to avoid suffering and death might be the pathway to experiencing it. A life established on the wrong answer would be your demise. It's quite a gamble, and it would be very costly to lose.

Better study up. Even if you don't dedicate your life to finding answers, it's at least worth considering. Honestly, a life founded on any answer would be costly if it were incorrect. All belief systems become destructive when they aren't rooted in …

Truth.

The greatest threat to all of us is the tyranny of falsehood. Tyranny is any oppressive government or rule that claims authority over your life. Every worldview, by its nature, claims authority. Even a worldview formed by postmodernism, which suggests there are many "truths," is—by nature—an authority. A culture that demands "you do you" is a defining rule of how you live your life. That means …

Every worldview functions as an objective solution to attaining the good life … to *true* life.

So which authority do you select? Which are worthy and which are tyrants?

This might be the part where I say it's time to choose, but you've already made your choice. The way you live your life is a reflection of the worldview you give authority.

And while we are talking about truth, here's another one …

You want to live a satisfying life.

Death is a certainty, but life is an option. How do we escape the captivity of mis-living?

Find truth.

Truth is the key to truly living. It is the cure to the destruction surrounding you. And where do we find truth? It depends on who you ask. There are a lot of opinions about what is right. But this is what the Bible says …

"Jesus said to the people who believed in him, 'You are truly my disciples if you remain faithful to my teachings. **And you will know the truth, and the truth will set you free.**'"[12]

The disciples were students of life. Their focus of study was learning how to live true, full lives. Jesus says by embracing his way of life—by applying his teachings—they will know *truth.*

In a world saturated with opinion, we have lost our ability to discern what is true or false. But if we believe that Jesus is trustworthy—if what he says is true—then God's holiness is a beacon that guides us toward truth and exposes what is false. Remember, holiness is right living. When we live the way Jesus instructs, we are orienting ourselves to reach our full potential—to experience the best possible life.

The pursuit of holiness is the pursuit of truth. And the pursuit of truth is the pursuit of holiness.

Living a holy life isn't one option among various alternatives; it's the one truth among multiple lies.

That means truth is a source. If you try to create your truth, you're really creating a lie. You can't preserve truth, but the truth can preserve you. You can't inform truth, but truth can inform you.

The point is this: truth only exists if it is objective—if it is true for all people. That means truth is the foundation for human life. The antithesis of human flourishing is living in opposition to the truth.

The problem isn't that truth is vanishing. It can't vanish and it never will. That's what makes it true. But the issue we face is covering the truth with lies by adding new "truths" that conveniently fit our agendas. We start to wonder if what is true for us might not be true for someone else.

So what can we look to as a universal standard?

No, You Can't Just Be a Good Person

I had a conversation with someone who was skeptical of faith and decided to become agnostic. He concluded that the nature of God couldn't be known; therefore, his aim was simply to be a good person.

So the question becomes: Can you be a good person without God?

Absolutely not.

Now slow down for a second because you may have misunderstood what I meant.

You might feel tempted to protest this statement and name several good people who don't believe in God. But don't worry; I can, too. I know lots of people that don't believe in God that easily align their lives in a way that the Bible would consider good. They are people who love others, are generous to those in need, serve people wholeheartedly, fight for justice, and work toward peace and reconciliation.

But this is why—despite however many good and decent non-believers exist—I stand behind this claim:

God is *necessary* in our understanding of what is good—whether you believe in him or not. God is the O-N-L-Y thing that can provide an objective standard of what is good. If God does not exist then we have no objective standard. Our morality is nothing more than a social construct. That would mean good and evil or right and wrong do not exist—and here's why ...[13]

When we say that something is good, we're making a claim that it is determined by what we believe is *true.* What we call "good" or "bad" are statements of fact. To use these labels is to assert them universally. If you think murder is "bad," you aren't allowing space for disagreement. You are saying that anyone who challenges this notion is *wrong.*

If there were no God, then what is "good" is subjective. It would be a matter of opinion. In that sense, everyone has the responsibility to decide for themselves what is good. But we all know that to let everyone decide what is good or bad for themselves would compromise a universal guideline. That's what we mean when we say we want to be good people.

We want to measure up to an objective standard.

This is why God is necessary. He defines what it means to be good. If you don't believe in God then here is the tough question you'll need to answer:

Who—or what—determines the standard of what is good?

If all people get to decide for themselves then you have no right to tell anyone what they are doing is wrong. Whatever you consider evil is your own opinion. This is problematic when you're trying to abide by a standard that you think should apply to everyone.

If you're trying to be good without God then you're likely just borrowing bits and pieces from the standard God has already established.

We all know "good" exists. It saturates the moments that make us grateful to be alive. It's the moment a child enters the world. It's receiving a college acceptance letter. It's attending a wedding. It's watching a sunset. It's sharing a bottle of wine with friends. It's watching a toddler take her first step. It's a puppy licking your face. It's hearing someone say *I love you.*

These things are good.

They are experiences of a universal force that permeates our world. You don't have to be told they are good. You know it because it's true.

We all know "bad" exists, too. It floods the moments that make us hate to be alive. It's the moment you discover your lover has cheated on you. It's finding out you were the victim of discrimination. It's when someone steals from you. It's when you're the target of vitriol on social media. It's when you're raped or molested. It's when someone tells you to kill yourself.

These things are bad.

They are things no one wants to experience. You don't have to be told they are bad. You know it because it's true.

Truth exists. But that doesn't mean you have to agree with it. It just means that anything contrary is false. Unfortunately, many people choose to live false lives. We get stuck rejecting the truth.

When this happens, God gives us a gift …

Conviction

When I was in elementary school I lived right across from the playground. On the weekends kids from the neighborhood would congregate and form an unsupervised recess, free of the oppressive teachers monitoring our actions or the thunderous bell calling us back to class.

One Saturday I made my way over to the basketball court between the swings and the jungle gym. My 5-year-old sister trailed behind, occasionally reminded by my annoyed expressions that her presence was unwanted.

It was never long before some kid caught sight of you from their window and rushed out to join. On this particular day, it was a girl just a year younger than me that accompanied us. After a few minutes, she became just as irritated, and together we ganged up on my sister with petty insults and teasing remarks.

It felt playful (at least for us) until this girl had an idea. She instructed my sister to cover her eyes and count to ten. I'd wondered if maybe she'd signal me to run and hide so my sister would cluelessly wander around the playground searching for us.

As my sister began counting I crouched down preparing to sprint, but I got no such signal. Instead, this girl just repositioned herself behind my sister and waited. Confused, I stood there watching. She placed a finger over her pursed lips commanding me to be quiet as she crouched down.

... 8 ... 9 ... 10.

By the time my sister opened her eyes, her pants had been pulled down to her ankles. She stood there on the basketball court in her underwear, quickly pulling her pants to her waist and nervously laughing it off.

This incident wasn't necessarily traumatic for my sister. Just stupid kids pulling stupid pranks. In fact, it's something she hardly remembers. But I do.

This crossed a line, and I enabled it. I took my little sister by the hand and told her it was time to go home.

I had always heard that we all have a conscience that helps us to know right from wrong. In that moment, mine was screaming obscenities at my complacency. I was ashamed that I allowed this action to take place.

The moment we got home I went to my room and cried into my pillow.

It's not a good feeling to know we've made a mistake. It's not a feeling we want, but it is most certainly something we need. It is a gift from God. The gift of …

Conviction.

Conviction is the sense that you've done something wrong. That there is a standard of what is good and right, and your decisions didn't measure up. We all have conviction at varying levels. We all have a sense of right and wrong.

Conviction is a good thing. It's able to open our eyes and sharpen our awareness when we begin to get off track. Conviction is the voice of reason, calling us to a higher standard. Conviction is the reminder that we aren't in step with who we're meant to be.

It's designed to function like the road ridges on the highway, alerting you that you're drifting outside the lines.

If we desire the presence of a holy God then we will feel conviction. We will begin to see our imperfections reflected through the lens of God's holiness. This isn't intended to drown us in guilt or make us feel worthless. But it's hard to have confidence in who God says we are when we feel so naked and ashamed. Remember, God wants to clothe us so we can live free from shame—but conviction is a necessary step in the process.

But now that we've established the role of conviction, there is another important question we need to ask …

What *informs* our convictions?

Let's say you grew up in a home where you were taught to lie, cheat, and steal. If that was your world, you wouldn't have any conviction against what you were doing. We all know there are people doing bad things they don't consider wrong. And before you start pointing the finger, you're one of those people. And so am I.

That's the problem—we learn at an early age to silence our proper convictions.

We can't simply rely on how we feel. We need to be taught the difference between right and wrong. And anything taught comes from a *source.*

So what source is reliable? What source is trustworthy? What source is perfect? What source is true?

What source is … holy?

The entire collected works of the Bible offer one unified answer …

God.[14]

God is the only source that can inform our convictions. It's not to bring us shame, it's to keep us safe from the dangers of our destructive behaviors and decisions. But we need to *condition* our convictions. We need to train them to align with God's Word and God's Spirit.

We need to feed them truth.

Paul writes this to the church in Rome:

> Don't copy the behavior and customs of this world, but let
> God **transform** you into a new person by changing the way
> you think. Then you will learn to know God's will for you,
> which is good and pleasing and perfect.[15]

I emphasized the word "transform" in this verse because it is the
most important one.

**When we allow our convictions to be shaped by God's holiness,
we are transformed into the people we are truly meant to be.**

One way or another, every day you're in the process of formation.
Every day of your life, something is shaping you. And given
enough time, that process—for better or for worse—is making you
into a new person.

You're either being formed by the patterns and customs of
your environment—moving with the current of society, or you're
deconstructing a false narrative to walk in line with the true path. The
one that directs you toward God's will, which is …

Good.

Pleasing.

Perfect.

Most of us would affirm a desire to be a good person. But the journey
toward holiness begins by admitting … **you are not good.**

You need to be transformed by the one who is. The one who can train
your convictions and align them with the truth.

If you want to be good, you have to start with God.

Stop Believing in God

I believed in Santa for a bit longer than the average person. I'm not sure at what age kids realize that the man who visits every house in one night is a myth, but I do remember the age there becomes division among the group. There comes a point when some lose their belief in Santa, and somewhere around this time, the consensus is split down the middle. And so the great debate ensues.

"Do you believe in Santa?"

When I reached this stage, I held tight to my faith in St. Nick. How else do the presents appear under the tree on Christmas morning? But the opposing view shook me. Toward the end, what remained of my faith was more wishful thinking than genuine belief. Sooner or later, we all see behind the curtain and stop believing in Santa.

Outside of a small dose of wonder, not much is lost when a kid no longer believes. Those who do aren't any different from the ones that don't. Perhaps the only practical function of a kid's belief in Santa is the narrow window when Christmas is approaching, and parents can leverage this belief for an incentive to behave.

Believing in Santa doesn't really distinguish kids in an obvious way.

When I first became a Christian at 13, I began asking my friends about their faith.

It was a one-question survey—*do you believe in God?*

If they said, "Yes," I was relieved. Good, I thought. They were going to heaven. If they said, "No," then they weren't. It was that simple. That was my metric for someone's eternal destiny. All you had to do was believe in God, and you were safe.

Which leads us to an important question: what does it mean to *believe* in God?

Early in faith, the answer was clear—you are simply affirming that God exists. There is more out there than what we can see. We aren't here by accident. This perspective informed my method of evangelism. I thought if I could just get people to say they thought God existed, they were a lock to get into heaven.

When I say it out loud, it's obvious how ridiculous this way of thinking is. We can call it for what it is—shallow and superficial. But this posture actually reflects the belief of a lot of people. Even though we are now living in a post-Christian society in America, there is still a large majority of the population that would affirm belief in God. Which means this:

There doesn't always seem to be a clear difference between those that believe in God and those that don't.

Do you see the problem here?

We all know that our beliefs should dictate our actions. If I sincerely believed that a tornado was going to rush through my neighborhood then that belief would determine my response. I would board up windows. I would collect essential and valuable items. I would gather my family underground. My actions would look very different than the people around me that didn't believe a tornado was going to rush through the neighborhood.

The fact remains that there are a lot of people that sincerely believe in God, but their belief *doesn't* change the way they live. They are sitting on the porch with the rest of their neighbors, watching the sky darken and feeling the winds picking up.

Our beliefs should influence the way we live. They should dictate our actions. They should create a foundation on which we stand. This is what Jesus says …

> *But anyone who hears and doesn't obey is like a person who builds a house right on the ground, without foundation. When the floods sweep down against that house, it will collapse into a heap of ruins.*[16]

In other words, if you believe in God, but live like the rest of the world—you're a fool.

That might sound harsh, but a lot of the Bible is purely focused on challenging foolishness with wisdom. Our belief is supposed to do something in us. It's supposed to take us somewhere. It's supposed to place us on a path toward holiness.

Either the things you believe will influence the way you live, or the way you live will influence the things you believe.

Don't simply hear what Jesus has to say—and don't simply *believe* that he said it.

Apply it. Live it. Do it. This is the only way we can experience the freedom of God's holiness.

Fear of God

I've always had a knack for making friends, but by no stretch of the imagination was I ever the "popular" kid.

When you're not the popular kid—and especially if you're the unpopular kid—you spend a lot of time imagining what life would be like to ascend the social ladder and stand among the people who score touchdowns, drive luxury cars, or set trends for the rest of the lowly no-name try-hards mimicking their every move.[17]

I would spend my days in class picturing myself walking into a room and feeling the weight of everyone's gaze, garnering admiration, praise, and jealousy. I wondered what it would feel like to have the confidence and assurance that if something worthwhile was happening, I'd be the first to get the invitation, instead of hearing about it the next day. I imagined having the power of seduction and knowing girls wanted to be with me. I dreamed of being a teenage celebrity, sifting through the crowds of people trying to get my attention.

Even if you never experienced this feeling to the same extreme, you have at least been in a circle of people that were praising someone while hoping you might be the subject of such admiration in another circle somewhere else.

But underneath that enthusiastic desire for praise is something we don't want. It's a gnawing fear that takes root in us and aims to command our thoughts and actions. It's the fear of ...

Judgment.

A judgment is an assessment made that is measured against a particular standard. Think of a panel of judges in a dance competition or at an Olympic event. Their role is to draw a conclusion of a participant's performance based on the highest standard. As she walks off stage or rises to the surface of the water, she awaits her score.

We are all surrounded by panels of judges. We are awaiting our score.

We all want to be liked. Which means we are all—at some level—afraid of being disliked.

We have a *fear* of judgment.

And not just from people. We fear the holy and perfect judgment of God.

If the thought of standing before the heavenly court while your life decisions are being evaluated through the lens of perfection doesn't make you a little nervous, then you probably need to spend some more time in self-reflection.

The Bible uses the phrase "fear of the LORD" a number of times. I've heard many pastors reduce that term to a metric of respect, but I think that downplays what the biblical authors describe.

Here's why ...

If you put me up close to a lion behind the glass of an exhibit at the zoo, I can say I have a healthy respect for the physical power of that lion. But it's easy to say that behind the safety of the glass.

If you suddenly drop me into the exhibit, I'm not just experiencing a sense of respect. I am now deeply afraid of personally experiencing that power and the consequence it would have on my well-being.

It is a fear of being destroyed. It's the same reason people run out of a burning building or sprint from grenades on the battlefield.

The fear that's fueling your instinct to flee is for your survival. It's how we protect ourselves.

And so, if you thought the lion was scary, imagine coming in contact with the creator of the universe, hell-bent on destroying sin.

It never says so in the Bible, but among the many people in Scripture that ever came close to God's presence, or encountered a heavenly messenger, I'd bet by the time they got up from the ground and back on their feet, there was a considerable pee stain on their pants. They are afraid of God because they know he could destroy them. But he doesn't.

Despite this appropriate reaction of fear, God's most common response is …

Do not be afraid.[18]

Fear is a powerful emotion, and it materializes in an infinite number of ways. We all create a long list of fears from the moment we're born. There are some that we conquer and some that conquer us. Some of our fears are the same and some are different.

But there is one thing they all have in common …

The perception of harm.

What we fear is something we believe will harm us, in some way, shape, or form. And so we take precautions. We distance ourselves from what we determine is threatening. We craft a suit of armor. We take the necessary measures to protect ourselves—physically, emotionally, mentally, and spiritually.

That's what makes this statement from God about fear so important.

When God says, "Do not be afraid," one of the layers of this statement is, "I wish you no harm."

When you're in his presence, you don't need to be on guard. You don't need to strap on a suit of armor for protection. You don't need to build up a wall and hide behind it. You don't need to cover yourself with a garment of fig leaves.

Often our fear is that when we encounter God's holiness, he will judge us, and his judgment will somehow harm us.

Here's the good news—God *has* judged you. **But his judgment doesn't bring harm. It brings healing.**

God has assessed you to the measure of his holy perfection, and you didn't score well. None of us have. Paul writes to the church of Rome, "We all fall short of God's glorious standard."[19]

That's why God sent us Jesus.

He accomplished something for us that we couldn't accomplish for ourselves. When we threw ourselves off the diving board, we hit the water with a thunderous crash. As we sank to the bottom of the pool, we knew what to expect from the judges when we resurfaced. But Jesus lifted us out of the water and pointed our attention to the official results ...

A perfect score.[20]

The Bible tells us when we place our trust in God, we don't need to fear him.

The Lord is my light and my salvation—
so why should I be afraid?
The Lord is my fortress, protecting me from danger,
so why should I tremble?[21]

But that's not to say our fear is unnecessary. It's just misplaced.

The real reason to be afraid isn't how Jesus will judge us, but rather, how we judge him.

Gabbatha

While Jesus prayed in the garden on the night before his betrayal, he also experienced the fear of judgment. He was afraid of how the judgment passed on him would bring him harm.

In an attempt to leverage the Roman government for their agenda, the religious leaders had Jesus brought before the Roman official Pontius Pilate for sentencing.

When Pilate heard the accusations against Jesus and saw the passion of the crowd, he determined that an aggressive flogging would settle the matter. When Jesus returned, Pilate was prepared to release him back to the public. But the Pharisees insisted that Jesus be put to death on the cross.

Reading this story today, we have the advantage of knowing the outcome. But Pilate didn't. He was faced with killing an innocent man or risking his political career.

So he had a decision to make. John 19 says this …

"Then Pilate sat down on **the judgment seat** on the platform that is called the *Stone Pavement* (in Hebrew, *Gabbatha*)."[22]

Did you notice that "Stone Pavement" was capitalized? That's because it's a proper noun. The architects of this ancient building, as well as the biblical authors, actually *named* the place where these kinds of decisions were made.

In Greek, the word is *Lithostrótos* and in Hebrew *Gabbatha*,[23] and both literally mean "an elevated stone pavement." I guess the general naming of things was a bit harder back then.

But *Gabbatha* is home to something else …

The judgment seat. The word used in greek is *bématos.* Another way to translate it is …

Throne.

In other words, Pilate walks up to the elevated platform to take a seat on the throne to make his judgment. And who is he judging?

Jesus.

When we read this passage in Scripture, it's easy to isolate it as a historical moment determined by a man of power thousands of years ago. But this isn't just a story of Pilate. It's a story about you.

Somewhere you have a *Gabbatha.* It's not a throne resting on a stone pavement in your house. It's the throne anchored in your heart. No one can set foot on your *Gabbatha.* It's the space where you're elevated and have the authority to make a decision.

Is Jesus guilty or innocent?

It's easy to criticize Pilate for compromising his integrity in order to maintain his position, but unfortunately, we often choose to condemn Jesus rather than stand with him as well.

That means the reason to be afraid isn't how God judges *us*. The reason to be afraid is how *we* judge God.

The fate of our life hinges on what we decide at *Gabbatha*. If you choose to condemn truth, it has devastating consequences for your life. This isn't God casting you out. It's you casting God out. It's rejecting the path he has set before you—to return to his presence and live in harmony with his will.

We may decide that it's easier to protect our status, desires, or comforts rather than embrace the truth of God. Like Pilate, we might compromise our integrity for the sake of appearances at the cost of betraying a holy man. We might sell our morals to the highest bidder instead of doing what is right.

That's why we need transformation: to relieve us of the heavy burden of making judgments and instead evaluate what we do by the standard of God's holiness.

If we don't, we will lose our ability to discern right from wrong. And if you can no longer tell right from wrong, you're in danger of becoming the bad guy …

The Red Lightsaber

Ever since I was young, I was a huge Star Wars fan. While other kids were out playing sports, I was practicing my lightsaber choreography with friends down the street. In our minds, we were becoming intimidating warriors through the disciplines of our training, but looking back, I think we were only successful at protecting our virginity.

For Star Wars fans, there is something about the way these movies and stories make you feel. Heroic tales of courageously battling against the forces of evil. Defiantly challenging the villains for the sake of a worthy cause. Mastering your skills to help others.

We were obsessed. These movies aided in our formation in profound ways. We wanted to be like these Jedi heroes on screen. We wanted to fight the bad guys—and there is one distinguishable quality of a Star Wars villain …

The red lightsaber.

Two characters approach one another. After an exchange of words and threats, each grabs the hilt on their waist. A duel is imminent. Both prepare by igniting their weapons. One is blue—good guy. One is red—bad guy. It's that simple.[24]

Unfortunately, it's not quite that easy to identify the bad guys in real life. We all know they exist.

The real question is—do *they* know they exist?

Is Darth Vader aware he is carrying a red lightsaber? Or worse, does he no longer recognize which colors signify good or evil?

Do villains self identify as villains?

In the movies, perhaps. It's easier for the audience to justify aggression and force when the antagonist wears their injustice like a badge of honor.

But what about in real life? Do the bad guys know they are bad? Unfortunately, when you're not on a Hollywood set and your surroundings don't include digital cameras, it becomes a lot harder to know the role you're playing.

The problem with any villain—real or fictional—is their ability to justify wrongdoing for the sake of their projected or desired outcome. We call this a blind spot.

And guess what?

You have them too. We all justify the methods or positions we take for our desired outcome.

Those seeds are planted in all of us. How do we know if we've let them grow in our hearts and minds? Most of us don't carry around lightsabers to check which color is glowing from our hand.

So how do you know if you're the bad guy?

Jesus uses this illustration …

> *A good tree can't produce bad fruit, and a bad tree can't produce good fruit. A tree is **identified by its fruit**. Figs are never gathered from thorn bushes, and grapes are not picked from bramble bushes.*[25]

The proof is in the pudding, as they say.[26] What you produce is the result of what is flowing through you. You are like a tree, contributing fruit in the environment where you have been planted. And producing fruit is inevitable. Like a tree, you can't prevent yourself from producing fruit. But unlike a tree, you can control the quality of the fruit you produce. You can choose to produce good fruit by living through God's Holy Spirit. This is the measure of good fruit produced …

"But the Holy Spirit produces this kind of fruit in our lives: love, joy, peace, patience, kindness, goodness, faithfulness, gentleness, and self-control."[27]

That means we should all be asking ourselves some questions:

What kind of fruit am I producing? What do people experience when they interact with me? What is said of me when I'm not around? Do others benefit from having me in their life?

I think most of us draw the conclusion that we're a good tree producing good fruit. But how will we know for sure?

If a tree is known by its fruit, then the fruit needs to be sampled. And here's the problem with self-assessment …

The tree doesn't taste the fruit.

That means you'll need humility because you aren't the one deciding if you're the good guy or the bad guy. You will need to remain open to the idea that what you're producing is bad. And that's a tough pill to swallow.[28]

If you want to know if you're growing toward holiness, you should begin by asking the people God has put in your life, "What kind of fruit have I been producing?" Seek it out. Inquire generously from people like you. Also from people not like you at all. From people that follow your leadership. From people that supervise you. From people that seem to like you. From people that seem to avoid you. From people that share your skin color. From people that don't share your skin color.

The people all around you—no matter how similar or different— are consuming the fruit you produce. Get their insight to measure its quality.

Good fruit is an indicator of right living.

War and Peace

Holiness is a declaration of war on evil. It's the process of conquering the territory in your life inhabited by your disordered desires.

War in any context is never desirable but sometimes necessary. It's a method of protecting and shepherding what you are responsible for. It's a method of defense when an enemy threatens to take your freedom.

Some wars are unjust and unnecessary. They are the manipulative conquests of a few to gain power. These wars—the ones that fuel sinful agendas—should be avoided at all costs.

But there is another war that should not be avoided. A war that demands your engagement.

This war isn't for land or resources or nation.

This war is for your *soul*.

Don't diminish this reality in the cushion of metaphor. War is violent, and this one is no different. It is brutal and gruesome. This battle is fought with an enemy that wishes to enslave you. That means identifying who the true enemy is:

> For we are not fighting against flesh-and-blood enemies, but against evil rulers and authorities of the unseen world, against mighty powers in this dark world, and evil spirits in the heavenly places.[29]

Jesus wasn't violent with humans. He gave up his life to protect them. Jesus wages his war on the forces of darkness.

Your enemy isn't the person who hurt you, the opposing political party, the people with different skin color, or some country you've never been to. The true enemy is a spiritual enemy, and in this war, you need to shoot to kill.

You are already on the frontlines of this war, whether you want to be or not. But there is an alternative to fighting. You don't have to engage in the battle. You can also consider …

Submission.

Fight or submit. Those are the only two options. Non-participation is the full victory of the enemy. To stay out of the fight means you've already lost it.

There is a great image of this in the movie *Braveheart.*

William Wallace—a man in an English-occupied Scotland—falls in love with a young woman from his childhood. During this time, the noblemen of Scotland attempt to recruit Wallace to join their rebellion against the tyrant King Edward Longshanks, who grants his men permission to conquer the land and the people of Scotland through tactics of violence and oppression.

Wallace initially declines the invitation to join his fellow Scots in an uprising against England. He wants to avoid war in favor of living in peace. He attempts to live a simple life hoping to go unnoticed by the oppressive Englishmen.

At first, his decision appears to be noble. Perhaps it is better to abstain from the war than to engage.

Many of us try the same approach. When something threatens us, it feels easier to slip into the background. To remain silent and hope we don't become a target. We think maybe we can wait out the war and arrive on the other side unharmed.

But it's not long before Wallace realizes that despite his efforts of avoidance, the war finds its way to him. The English attempt to rape his wife and later have her killed.

It's a tragic moment in the movie, but an important revelation for Wallace. He finally sees there is no way to live in peace with an enemy that seeks to destroy everything you love. The longer you avoid the battle for liberation, the more that is taken from you.

This serves as a picture of what is happening at a spiritual level, and this is what we need to realize …

There is no way to live in peace with the *true* enemy. The longer you attempt to withdraw from this war, the more that will be taken from you. The enemy will conquer more territory in your heart. The enemy will cut off more life-giving resources that allow you to thrive. The enemy will seize your relationships and leave you in isolation. The enemy will police your thought process and limit your perspective.

Once Wallace resolves to engage in battle, he is able to unite his people under one cause. The cause proclaimed in his final breath is …

Freedom.

You cannot abstain from the war for your soul. There is no philosophy of mutual respect. No "live and let live." The Adversary comes to kill, steal, and destroy.

HOLY

You can't have a rich and satisfying life if you won't
confront the enemy.

Fight or die.

But *how* you fight may not be as you'd expect. This war isn't about
suiting up and charging toward an army of demons led by Satan.

This battle is fought *with* yourself, *within* yourself.

The enemy's tactic is to invade your heart and your mind and hope
you do nothing. To convince you to be passive. The battle isn't a show
of strength to see who is stronger. That battle has already been lost.
Humans were defeated long ago. That's why we're in this mess now.

The battle is actively allowing the Spirit to take over our lives and fight
this enemy with the strength we don't have … but God does.

Even though we face spiritual battles against the forces of darkness,
this remains the point of the physical battles of the Bible: God will fight
for his people. Look at the story of Jericho in the book of Joshua.
After the time of Moses, Joshua leads his people to Canaan, the
land promised to Abraham and his descendants. Before he gathers
his people, Joshua encounters a soldier, which we are told is an
angel of the LORD.

Joshua asks the man, "Are you for us or for our enemies?"[30]

"Neither" the angel replied.

Neither?

Wait, I thought God was for his people? Isn't that what this
story is about?

This is important because it serves as a reminder to be cautious. The
people we consider our enemies aren't necessarily God's enemies.

We want to know if God is for *us,* but the question from this story asks—are you for *God?* Are you pushing your own agenda, or are you aligning with his?

To solidify that point, the angel gives Joshua these instructions …

For six days, march around the city. On the seventh day, march around the city seven times, with the priests blowing the trumpets … then the wall of the city will collapse, and the army will go up, everyone straight in.[31]

That's the plan? I mean, we all know nobody likes jazz, but it's not enough to make a city crumble. Why not just attack like normal people?

Because the victory doesn't belong to Israel. They don't win the battle. God does.

This isn't intended to be a mere outline of history. There is a message that transcends this particular battle to inform the one you are fighting, and here it is:

You are outmatched. The enemy is insurmountable. You don't have the resources or the strength to gain an advantage in this war. There is no hope for a victory at the work of your hands. But God fights in your place, and he will not be defeated. Trust in him to deliver you from the enemy.

If the people would have accepted this truth early on, there would have been a lot less war in the Bible.

You aren't stronger than the enemy. But God is. That's why we let him fight on our behalf. The method of accomplishing this is to grant God permission to enter our hearts and minds so that he can eradicate the darkness and rebuild from the destruction of the enemy's invasion.

That's what transformation is—becoming someone different. Becoming someone filled with God's Spirit. We win the war by allowing God to fight for us. When we invite God's presence into our lives, he is expelling the presence of darkness.

Paul writes, "For once you were full of darkness, but now you have light from the Lord. So live as people of light! For this light within you produces only what is good and right and true."[32]

To accept Jesus as Lord is to turn on a light in your heart and mind and watch the darkness flee.

Next time you're in a dark room, flip the light switch and watch the darkness dissolve as the light chases it out of the room. If you were able to see the speed of light, when you flip the switch, you'd watch a beam of light beginning at the source stretching out to every area of the room, swallowing up the darkness as it travels.

This is the image of Jesus. Eliminating darkness wherever he goes, faster than you can see it happening.

Accepting Jesus as Lord is like installing a light bulb in your heart and mind and listening for the Spirit to guide you in the darkness toward the switch when you can't see.

The enemy has already invaded. You can submit, or you can fight. And remember, there can be no peace. Your soul is on the line.

A Holy Seed

Have you ever gotten in trouble because someone tattled on you?

You had to be cautious when you were around tattle-tales because they volunteered for the role of morality police. If they saw you doing something wrong, they wouldn't hesitate to inform you of the rules and threaten to expose you to the proper authorities.

In a lot of ways, that's how people viewed the prophets of the Bible.

They were responsible for delivering a message from God—specifically when his people were drifting from his commands of holy living with instructions on how to correct their course. It was a difficult job and required confronting people about their behavior.

Many of them were viewed as community hall monitors.

But their role was crucial for God's plan of transforming his people. He used them to speak out against the people's pride and stubbornness and offer the necessary warnings when they wandered into trouble.

There were many prophets, but one named Isaiah had a vision and a message that changed everything.

In his vision, Isaiah is standing in the Temple of God's presence, and he's terrified that he will be destroyed. But God takes burning coal and places it on his lips and declares, "See, this coal has touched your lips. Now your guilt is removed, and your sins are forgiven."[33]

God *purifies* Isaiah.

Isaiah is able to stand before God, not because of something he did, but because of something God did. Isaiah is made clean in God's presence. In order to become holy, God needs to burn away our impurities. We normally associate fire with hell, but the journey toward holiness is preparing us for the fires of heaven.[34]

For the record, I don't think God is nudging us to walk the plank and dive headfirst into a sea of flames. But I do believe that the process of purification is, at least, very uncomfortable, if not decidedly painful. That's made clear by the end of Isaiah's vision.

God tells him to inform the people they have turned away from him and no longer know who they are. They are like a tree that has grown strongly rooted in their sin, which means they will be cut down. Yet another painful image, and not a fun message to deliver.

But that's not all. This is where God also provides hope.

He says the stump that remains will be a *holy seed.*[35]

A stump is a sign of death. It serves as a reminder that at one point, a tree stood tall, and now it's gone. But inside of that stump, rooted in the death of the tree, is a sign of new life. It is the possibility of growth. It's a seed, but it's no ordinary seed …

This seed is *holy.*

Some things need to be cut down. They need to be destroyed because they are inhibiting the growth of something good. When God chops down our ways of living, it exposes something inside of us that wasn't allowed to grow. It exposes a holy seed—that when properly planted— enables us to become who we truly were meant to be.

We have all built a life rooted in pride, stubbornness, and compromise. And Jesus comes marching through the forest like a lumberjack to chop it down. That's why he says, "The time has come … the kingdom of God has come near. **Repent** and believe the good news!"[36]

I don't usually use the word "repent" in casual conversation. It feels like it's supposed to be reserved for significant religious epiphanies or shouted from megaphones by angry street preachers to inform you that you're going to hell.

Repentance feels like when you go to the church altar and plead with God on hands and knees to forgive you for some mistake you've made. Repentance feels like when you're soaking the floor in tears because you can't bear the weight of your guilt and shame. Repentance feels like humbly approaching God to remind him of how terrible you are.

But that isn't what Jesus is saying. The word translated "repent" comes from the Greek word *metanoeó,* which means "to change one's mind or purpose."[37]

That paints a slightly different picture.

That's not to say there isn't a time and place for us to have a moment of awakening that breaks us to the core and drops us to our knees. That's an appropriate reaction to an encounter with a holy God.

But when Jesus is preaching his message, he's telling people to simply *change their minds.* Change their outlook. Change their perspective. Change their goal. Change their path.

Turn around … you're going the wrong way.

Jesus isn't threatening or intimidating. His message is like a road sign warning you of danger ahead. And the appropriate reaction to a road sign is gratitude. Its purpose is to keep you alert and safe.

And every road sign is there for a reason. No one is driving around with a stack of signs, randomly cementing them on the side of the road as they go along. Every sign you pass was placed with a purpose. It's a brief visual message that there are things you should watch out for—railroads, deer crossing, falling rock, winding road.

All of these signs were placed by someone at some point because they were relevant. They pointed to real, practical dangers.

Jesus' message of repentance is a signpost to warn us of the practical dangers we need to watch out for. He's letting us know that he's traveled the road ahead, and it contains some major pitfalls if we don't proceed with caution and intentionality.

He's saying, "Don't wait. The time is now. Change your mind and believe. Align yourself with a different way of life. Watch out for the dangers ahead."

Holiness begins with the deconstruction of the self. When Isaiah tells the people they will be cut down, it's going to hurt. But God will begin to grow something from the wound that will produce right living.

Being cut down in our pride and arrogance is an act of mercy for God to offer healing and plant the holy seed for a new life.

Milk Is for Babies

When we had our first child, we spent time several evenings in the months leading up to delivery taking a birthing class in the hospital. It was exciting (and nerve-wracking) to learn the information needed to care for your new baby.

We wanted to know everything, or so I thought. Apparently, there are a lot of things I eventually discovered I had no desire in knowing.

But among the information that made me queasy, there was an interesting portion dedicated to feeding your newborn baby.

Did you know that when a baby latches on to her mother for breastfeeding, there are chemical receptors that communicate, through her body, the levels of nutrients that are needed for the baby's next feeding? This information is sent through the baby's saliva to produce exactly what is needed for healthy, nutritional growth and development.

How this happens is simply incredible. But *why* this happens is worth some extensive consideration. Why is there this connection between baby and mother?

Because it's what's needed for the species to thrive; if it weren't for a mother's ability to produce milk for her baby, then it would die. Milk provides something *essential.*

There are two things we need to know about milk.

1) Milk is for babies.

It supports them. It meets their needs. It nourishes and sustains them. When a baby cries out in hunger to their mother, it's because their life depends on it.

The Bible uses this exact illustration to show us something about our spiritual development.

Like newborn babies, you must crave pure spiritual milk so that you will grow into a full experience of salvation. Cry out for this nourishment, now that you have had a taste of the Lord's kindness. [38]

As a parent, my desire is to get my kids to stop crying, but Peter is encouraging it. He says we need to have a posture where we are screaming for what only God can give us. God is able to feed us to the measure of our true needs. And once we get a taste, we cry out for more—like a hysterical infant in need of another meal.

And here's the connection, just so you don't miss it…

This is what holiness is.

A source of sustenance that nourishes and strengthens us. When we consume it, we are able to grow into a full experience of salvation. Holiness is what prepares us for God's kingdom. And not just when we die. Here and now. Holiness is what Jesus describes when he speaks of a rich and satisfying life. Holiness fills us with love and peace in our pains of fear and anxiety.

Holiness is consuming the truth and trusting in who God says we are. In how God made us to be. Holiness is the way our brokenness is healed. Holiness is the way we are made whole.

God desires to clothe our nakedness and vulnerabilities and insecurities in his righteousness to make us like him—to make us …

Holy.

Our walk with Jesus is a journey toward holiness, and the holiness of God will sustain and nurture us.

But here's the other thing the Bible wants to tell us about milk …

2) Milk is for babies.

Just as a newborn weans off of milk to solid food, we need to grow into a higher, more balanced diet that supports our continued growth and development.

Paul confronts the stunted growth of the Christians in Corinth by writing these words …

> I had to feed you with milk, not with solid food because you weren't ready for anything stronger. And you still aren't ready, for you are still controlled by your sinful nature.[39]

Even though milk provides what is needed for the young, it isn't a sustainable source of nutrition as time passes. Eventually, infants need to graduate from milk to solid food. That's true physically and spiritually.

In the spiritual realm, this progression is intended to strengthen our discipline and self-control —allowing us to escape the captivity of our sinful nature. We need to outgrow our disordered desires to reach our full potential. God's holiness will feed you and sustain you and nurture you, but over time a little bit isn't enough. Your stomach expands, and you need more than when you were young.

How do you know if you're moving from milk to solid food? What's the sign that would indicate your growth and development?

You can self assess your progression toward holiness by honestly answering this question:

Who—or what—has control over you?

You might be inclined to think you are in control—but you're wrong.

According to the Bible, there are two opposing wills that battle within you. The will of the Spirit and the will of the flesh—the sinful nature.

What you do is the result of which of these wills you allow to channel themselves through you. You're either controlled by the Spirit, or you're controlled by sin. Pauls writes this in Romans, "So letting your sinful nature control your mind leads to death. But letting the Spirit control your mind leads to life and peace."[40]

When two warriors do battle, they are both trying to impose their will over the other. The victor is the stronger of the two. Spiritual development is about lending your strength to the will of the Spirit instead of the will of the flesh.

Even if you're not in control, you're certainly in charge of deciding who is.

If you have ever felt stuck in your spiritual development, or maybe your relationship with God hit a wall, it's likely because you're holding on to something you need to move beyond. Paul's words are direct and might seem confrontational, but the alternative to growth and development is, at best, stagnancy and, at worst, regression to the point of decay.

The point is this: **we need to be growing in our journey toward holiness.**

God will sustain us with spiritual milk to meet our needs, but we must eventually move on to solid food. The sign that this is happening in our lives is when we are no longer controlled by our sinful nature.

But don't feel discouraged. God is exercising his grace in your development. There is room to be in process. Apprenticeship to Jesus is a marathon, not a sprint.

Perfectly in Process

The concept of overnight success is appealing. It's the idea that you apply yourself in a new way, in a new arena, and boom! You're a success. Maybe you're a natural talent or just fell into the right opportunity.

That's what we may assume when someone we've never heard of suddenly pops up in every late-night show interview, magazine cover, or news headline. There was a time when no one knew who Justin Bieber or Mark Zuckerberg were. Then as if with the flip of a switch, they became household names.

But the truth is overnight success is a myth. Behind anyone that suddenly rises to the top or is celebrated for their revolutionary accomplishments are countless hours of hard work, dedication, failure, and disappointment.

Most of the time, you just see the results, which is why I love documentaries that highlight someone's journey to success. We're all used to seeing these people in nice clothes, fancy cars, and surrounded by screaming fans. But if you ever get to see the home videos or photos from before their success, you realize, before they made it, they were just normal people working hard to achieve their dreams.

Those were the invaluable moments of preparation.

Right now, the results awaiting you are a product of your preparation. There's an old expression: if you fail to prepare, then you're preparing to fail.

If that's true, then at this very moment, you're preparing for something. Whether it's for the results you desire is a matter of intentionality, but either way, you will reap what you sow.

This doesn't bode well for those of us conditioned to expect immediate gratification. If you ever want to measure how much you struggle with this, just keep a personal emotional assessment when your food takes longer than expected to arrive at your table.

Sometimes we mistake the passing of time with our preparation. Suddenly the date arrives, and we expect results because we simply waited. Let's say you want to run a marathon—because you're a crazy person—and sign up for a race that's a few months out.

If you want to finish, you need to train. You need to prepare. And it requires you to get off the couch. If those months are spent binge-watching Netflix and eating chips and pizza, then on race day, you have perfectly prepared to go as far as you'll go—which won't be very far.

Good preparation is the process of equipping yourself to do something later that you are unable to do now.

The same is true of our faith journey. When I became a Christian, I thought I would suddenly become this great person that lived like Jesus. I expected overnight success, and it didn't happen. But just like all things we desire, our path toward holiness will not arrive at our feet. It is a long journey that requires training and preparation.

There are still many more failures, regrets, and mistakes ahead. Today you and I aren't perfect. But if we open more and more of our life to Jesus, then we are …

Perfectly in process.

That's why God offers us grace.

But grace has a purpose. Wherever God offers us grace, it's in a place he wants to move us beyond. Here's what I mean …

A few months ago, I was with my three-year-old son at the park, and there was another kid that wanted to play catch with us. After a few minutes, the attention span of both kids wore thin, and they became distracted. While the other kid had his head turned, my son remembered the game and picked up the ball, throwing it directly to the side of his head.

Tears instantly sprung from the kid's eyes like a fountain, and I tried to act quickly to comfort him. After things calmed down, I knew this was a parenting opportunity and explained to my son that, even though it was not his intent, he needed to apologize.

The timidly whispered, "Sorry" ensued.

The other kid responded, "It's okay."

Before I allowed them to continue, I gently asked my son's friend to rephrase.

"It's not okay," I assured him, directing my instruction to my son. "But if you're grateful he apologized and want to continue playing together, you can say, 'Thank you for your apology.'" And so he did.

Walking away from this exchange, I realized how often I do the same thing. I couldn't count the times I was on the receiving end of an apology coming from someone that wronged me in some way—to which I responded, "It's okay."

Isn't the whole point of an apology that something *wasn't* okay?

But I understand why I do this. Sometimes it feels awkward to receive an apology. It feels more comfortable to bend the truth to bring reconciliation. Let bygone be bygone.

For a long time, this was my understanding of God's grace. I make a mistake. I later apologize to God. He says *it's okay*—because he's a "nice" God—and then life goes on as normal. Which means life goes on … the same.

I'm preparing to make the same mistakes and later make the same apologies.

In our pursuit of transformation, there are a lot of mistakes ahead. God is aware of how much work needs to be done, and his grace allows us the room to grow.

But just because we receive grace from God doesn't mean he's telling us it's okay. In fact, if we are receiving his grace, it's not.

Hanging in the Balance

Let's take a look at an important story from the life of Jesus. As his ministry gained more attention, he was increasingly perceived as a threat by the religious leaders. And so they tried to arrange several theological traps to get him to slip up and say something errant in order to harm his reputation and credibility.

On one such occasion, they manage to catch a woman in adultery. Whatever methods they were able to do so are questionable, to say the least, but they aren't the ones on trial in this story. And neither is the woman.

Jesus is.

They bring this woman out in public before Jesus and challenge him to navigate a sentencing. According to the law—which is a reflection of God's uncompromising holiness and moral purity—this woman (and whomever she was with) had sinned. And sin, because it brings destruction, is therefore punishable by death. In fact, because the wage of sin is death, any sin is punishable by death against God's holy and perfect law.

But here's the issue: if all have sinned, who is qualified to carry out such a sentencing?

Which is the exact problem Jesus brings to the religious leaders.

"All right, but let the one who has never sinned throw the first stone!"[41]

If you notice, Jesus gives them permission to stone her. According to Jesus, the law isn't wrong. Sin is an abomination against God. It destroys God's creation. Everyone who sins should die for their crimes. That includes you and me.

But wait, that's crazy, right? I know I wouldn't sit idly by if I were in court and given the death sentence. Sure, I've made some mistakes. But do I deserve to die for them?

Perhaps we can appeal for …

Grace.

That sounds good to all of us, especially if it's to avoid capital punishment. It's almost like we came up with the idea ourselves. But as convenient as is for us, humans were not the authors of grace.

This was *God's* idea.

Since none of the accusers fall into the category of holy sinless perfection, they drop their rocks and leave one by one. They lack the credibility to carry out justice on behalf of God's holy law. And certainly, no one is willing to throw stones at themselves.

But according to the Bible, Jesus was sinless. He's the one that is able to carry out such a sentencing with uncompromising integrity. Now that all the religious leaders have gone, he's left to deal with the woman himself.

"Where are your accusers? Didn't even one of them condemn you?"
"No, Lord," she said.
And Jesus said, **"Neither do I. Go and sin no more."**[42]

There is something momentous happening in this passage that we can't afford to miss. **Jesus demonstrates the perfect balance between grace and truth.**

When Jesus says to the woman that he doesn't condemn her, he is giving *grace*. Grace is the unmerited favor of God to forgo judgment and condemnation. Jesus had the right to judge her, but instead, he chose an alternative—to save her from death.

But why? Why would Jesus offer grace if he is holy, perfect, and just? That's a good question, but here's a better one …

What does grace *accomplish* for those that receive it?

This is the question that gives us insight into what Jesus is doing in this story. Grace begins to paint a picture of a different reality. What if instead of death, people were given new life? What if instead of an ending, they could receive a new beginning? What if instead of seeing what someone became, we could help them see what they could become?

A fresh start. A new day. A reset. This is something every human craves because it's something every human needs.

You need grace. I need grace. Every person for all of human history needs grace.

Where do we find it?

There is no better case made than Jesus. In your worst moment, ripped out in the open, on display for others to see—naked and exposed, vulnerable and insecure—Jesus leaves the heavy rocks on the ground. He's telling you what he tells this woman …

I don't condemn you.

I. Don't. Condemn. You.

Grace arrives with a question—what if things could be different? What if people could be different? What if this grace could somehow transform people from who they've been into who they were created to be? It's a start, but it's not the destination.

Grace—although beautiful and inspiring—isn't enough to help you reach your true potential.

We still need a map. A compass. Something to guide us away from the captivity we've been freed from and toward the vision of freedom that held our hearts captive.

Grace is the antidote to the poison in our cup. But now we need a new cup, or we'll drink from the poison again.

Grace is necessary, but we still need something else.

This is why Jesus tells the woman to *go and sin no more.* The woman doesn't only need grace. She needs direction. She needs a path to lead her out of the pit she's fallen in. She needs …

Truth.

Grace can help you see a new world. But truth is how you step in and feel it. Both are essential—grace … and truth. And hanging in the balance?

Jesus. Or should we say hanging on a wooden cross? What Jesus' death symbolized in his sacrifice is perfect harmony of grace and truth.

The truth of the deadly consequence of sin. The grace of an opportunity for new life.

When you can truly understand the significance of this story, you'll realize God is good.

But good isn't a good enough word.

What do you call a God that is so good he's beyond imagination? What do you call a God that is so good he's unlike anything else that could be experienced? What do you call a God that is so good he draws you into relationship for blessing, regardless of what you've done or who you've been?

What do you call a God that is *too good* to just be called *good?*

Is there a word for that?

Yes. That word is *kadash*—set apart. Unique. Unlike anything else.

That word is …

Holy.

And something holy needs a home.

It's time to start building a …

PART V

TEMPLE

|*tem·ple*| |tem-pəl|
Noun

1   A building devoted to the worship or regarded as the dwelling place, of a god or gods or other objects of religious reverence.

2   (The Temple) either of two successive religious buildings of the Jews in Jerusalem. The first (957-586 BC) was built by Solomon and destroyed by Nebuchadnezzar; it contained the Ark of the Covenant. The second (515 BC-AD 70) was enlarged by Herod the Great from 20 BC and destroyed by the Romans during a Jewish revolt; all that remains is the Western Wall.

Booby Traps

When I was a kid, movies and cartoons taught me I'd have to prepare for a regular encounter with booby traps. Step on the loose stone, pull the wrong lever, or lean against the rigged wall, and you'll be dodging poison darts, hurtling shooting spears, or sprinting to roll under a lowering steel door.

I've since realized some of these meticulous contraptions are a bit impractical, but that doesn't take away from the reason for their existence.

I mean, why would anyone set up a bunch of booby traps anyway?

The answer is obvious: they are *protecting something.*

A special map. A rare treasure. A powerful relic.

Whatever it is, it's valuable enough to be fatally guarded. Even though your life hangs on the line, with every survived step, you can be assured you're getting closer to the prize. The more dangerous the obstacle, the nearer the reward.

And if those movies and cartoons were an accurate indicator, you knew the greatest treasures were found in …

A temple.

But this isn't just the makings of adventure fantasy or Hollywood blockbusters. Throughout history, temples were well known for the treasures they kept inside. And it makes sense when you come to understand why a temple is constructed in the first place.

Temples were sacred buildings dedicated to serving the gods for two reasons: appeasing their anger and garnering their favor.

When you're an insignificant, powerless human at the mercy of some mighty deity, you might live in fear of making him (or her) angry. It's a legitimate concern. Say the wrong thing, do the wrong thing, or think the wrong thing and ... ZAP. You suffer months of drought, your house is demolished by an earthquake, or your aunt Karen drops dead.

So how do you avoid these kinds of outbursts? How do you make a god happy? How do you receive their favor?

You build a temple. You fill it with valuables. You sacrifice your best stuff. And maybe if you say the right things, do the right things, and think the right things then ... ZAP. You yield a fruitful harvest, your wife becomes pregnant with a son, or your aunt Karen drops dead.

A temple was built as a demonstration of the splendor and glory of the god it served. That meant the taller the structure, the greater the expanse of land, the more valuable the materials, the bigger the treasure, and so on, the more favor you could conjure.

It was thought to be a simple transaction. When something bad happened in your life, you must have made a god angry. When something good happened, you must have made a god happy. You live in a constant cycle of receiving their anger and their favor.

Maybe that's how you think of the God of the Bible. An aggressive, temperamental being with nothing better to do than to watch your every move and keep a finger on the trigger ready to blast, or to bless.

If that's how you feel, then you've probably spent a good portion of your life walking the tightrope—trying to do all the right things and avoid all the wrong ones.

As you can imagine, as time went on—and as misfortune and disasters occurred—new temples were constructed all the time. But there were many gods to choose from. How do you know which temple was dedicated to which god?

Well ... you'd need an image. Some sort of sculpture or likeness made to reflect the god you were serving. You'd need to craft an idol that served as a placeholder for the god of that temple.

Now, there were many ancient temples, including one constructed by the Israelites. But the temple designed for Yahweh had one unique difference from the other temples of the pagan gods.

It wasn't known for what was inside but rather … what *wasn't*.

"Do not make idols or set up carved images, or sacred pillars, or sculptured stones in your land so you may worship them. I am the LORD your God."[1]

Where other temples were filled with idols crafted by worshipers, the Jewish Temple had none.

But why does this matter? Why does God make this commandment?

To answer this question, we need to talk about tents.

From Tabernacle to Temple

Up to this point, I've avoided discussing one of the most critical concepts in the Bible …

The Tabernacle.

Parts I-IV have allowed us to explore our insecurities, hope for our future, understand the God who pursues us, and begin walking the path to wholeness. But all of these things culminate in this final section where we dig into the idea of the Temple.

Soon after Moses leads the Israelites out of slavery from Egypt, he goes up to the top of a mountain to meet with God. Here, he receives the ten commandments, which function as an essential foundation to guide this new nation.

It outlines how these newly freed people ought to live in order to be in harmony with God and one another. How to build a strong community. How to live with meaning and purpose. How to live a rich and satisfying life.

These become the blueprints for a new way of living. A way that is different from the other nations who serve other gods.

Moses asks if the people are willing to abide by these guidelines and obey God's commands, and they agree. So Moses goes back up the mountain by himself while the people wait at the base, and God tells him something very important.

"Have the people of Israel build me a holy sanctuary ...."

Ohh ... of course! Because all the gods want a temple, right? How well you build the temple is how they decide if they will give you their anger or their favor.

It's the same old story. This isn't anything new. We all know the drill. Build a structure and fill it with valuables so God will be happy and maybe consider doing good things for us.

Later on, we get a very clear and detailed list of how this sanctuary should be constructed. It outlines the measurements, the furnishings, the materials. Passages like these are about as exciting as the owner's manual that came with your car. Chances are you probably threw it away or stuffed it in the glove box "just in case." Spoiler alert: even if you're broken down on the side of the road, you'll never use it.

The same is true for just about every Bible verse that describes the specifications of how this sanctuary needs to be built. None of them will make the cut for your Instagram bio.[2]

But as seemingly irrelevant as these instructions are, they are directing the people to build the Tabernacle—the mobile Temple of the Israelite people. Every god has a temple, and so these instructions were familiar in this ancient culture.

But Yahweh makes a clear distinction. What's more important than *how* this sanctuary is to be built is *why.*

"… so I can live among them."[3]

Where other temples are built to appease the gods who are thought to be somewhere far away, this Tabernacle is built so God can live in community with his people. Where other temples housed engraved lifeless idols, this Tabernacle housed the very presence of the divine force that spoke the universe into existence.

This is the plan because it's always been the plan. This is the vision because it's always been the vision. From the moment Adam gasped for oxygen with the breath of life until the world eventually fades into darkness and ashes, God is working to make his home among his people. He's bringing us back to a time when we walked freely with him in the garden.

Other temples are built because the gods are angry and stingy.

This temple is built so that God can live among his people and bless them.

Which is really another way of saying that this God wants to be *with* us.[4]

This Temple isn't built to distract God from his anger or manipulate him into giving us something we want. This Tabernacle is a *home*. God's presence will dwell within the center of this liberated community.

If that is true, then it tells us something else we need to know …

God's presence has the ability to fill space and time—it is available to his people and manifests in a physical way. God's presence is working to go somewhere—to *be* somewhere.

And so, when construction of the Tabernacle is complete, God takes his first steps inside. A cloud covers the Tabernacle, and it is filled with God's glory. It's a pretty big moment but maybe not for the reasons you think.

"The cloud of the Lord hovered over the Tabernacle during the day, and at night fire glowed inside the cloud *so the whole family of Israel could see it.*"[5]

As much as that might sound like a scene from Harry Potter, it has some important theological significance. Here's a question that has been asked for all of time: If God promises to live with his people, *how do you know he is there?*

The cloud of smoke and fire are **physical manifestations** of God's presence. It's God's way of saying, "You don't have to wonder where I am. You can see that I am with you."

In a world full of gods and temples, how do you know which one to serve? And when you serve them, how do you know what you're doing is working? How do you know if they are pleased or angry? How do you know if they are for you or against you?

This tribe of former slaves doesn't have to wonder. God assures them of his presence. And God's presence is a statement ...

I am *with* you.

This is a re-merging of heaven and earth. It isn't to say God's presence is *confined* to this space. As the Tabernacle passes from generation to generation, it later becomes a Temple made by King Solomon, who asks, "But will God really live on earth? Why even the highest heavens cannot contain you. How much less this Temple I have built!"[6]

God isn't *trapped* in this structure. The Tabernacle—and later the Temple—are **symbols.**

They are intended to reflect the image of the Garden of Eden—when we walked with God and were not ashamed to be naked. When fear and shame and insecurity didn't exist because we knew we were loved, and we were made holy in his presence.

The Jewish Temple stood in rebellion to other temples. It was a beacon of hope and light for the Israelites for a specific purpose: **to point the world to Yahweh.** This was how God fulfilled the covenant he made with Abraham. This was how he would bless the tribe of Israel. He would live among his people, and his presence would bring renewal. And not just for the Jews. This was also how God was going to bless all nations.

In a world searching for truth and meaning and purpose, the Temple is where others came to know God—and in him, find true life.

In that case, the next step is obvious.

We need *more* temples like this one. Temples that aren't like the other temples. Temples that are full of God's presence. Temples that aren't full of …

Idols.

The Thing About Idols

The Bible contains various genres of literature. Just like your local bookstore, your Bible has sections of history, poetry, memoir, self-help, fiction, non-fiction, and so on. We could spend countless hours diving into each book's historical context, literary methods, archaeological evidence, geographic location, but there are other books for that. Knowing *how* they were written is important, but for no greater reason than discerning *why* they were written, which is this:

To help direct humans toward proper worship.

This isn't exclusively why all of the Bible exists, but it's certainly why some—if not most—of it exists. Scripture is a guide to help humans align themselves with a correct posture of worship in thoughts, words, and actions.

It's human to worship. It is how we were created. We all worship something, even if you don't believe in God. Worship is elevating something as the subject of your devotion and allegiance.

This isn't a religious practice. It's a human practice.

If you elevate something and offer it your affection, then it will draw you in closer. Worship takes you somewhere. It's the strongest gauge of where you're going. That means what you worship becomes the trajectory of where your life is headed. It is an indicator of who you are becoming.

That's why the first two commandments given to the community of God's people deal with their posture of worship.

> I am the LORD your God, who rescued you from the land of Egypt, the place of your slavery. You must not have any other god but me. You must not make for yourself an idol of any kind or an image of anything in the heavens or on the earth or in the sea.[7]

To summarize: no gods; no idols. But what do they have to do with worship? Let's break it down a bit.

The Hebrew word for God is *Elohim*. It's also the Hebrew word for gods—as in little "g" god. The word for "God" and the word for "gods" is identical. So, practically this passage reads, "I am Yahweh *Elohim,* you shall have no other *elohim* before me." That seems to suggest you can take your pick of elohim in the cosmos.

Maybe you'd expect the Bible to say something more like, "I am Yahweh *Elohim.* There are no other *elohim,* so don't bother worshiping them …."

But it doesn't.

So here is the main reason for God's first commandment.

There are spiritual beings that aren't worthy of your worship. There are other spiritual agendas that conflict with Yahweh and his plan for creation. And worshiping something that is unworthy will always lead you down a dark path.

So what makes Yahweh worthy of their worship?

Before God gives the commandment, he gives the qualifier. Yahweh *rescued* the Israelites from their slavery. He is worthy of their devotion because he cares for them. He loves them. He goes to battle for them. He has a plan for them. He is with them.

Okay, I get the first commandment. It makes sense that we aren't worshiping the wrong spiritual beings. But why is this second one so important?

This is a good question, and some of the answers can be a bit complicated, but this second commandment is a warning.

When a human carves an idol, they are literally forming the image of the god they are creating. Therein lies the problem. Human beings were created to bear the image of God; he should be forming us, we shouldn't be forming him.

There's an old adage: In the beginning, God made humans in his own image, and they've been returning the favor ever since. It's cliche, but it articulates an important concept.

Worship refines us into the image of *what* we worship, which is why it's so dangerous when we worship an image we've crafted ourselves.

The second commandment is about reorienting the people away from their disordered desires and aligning with God's will. He's letting them know he can't be formed or shaped like wood or stone or clay. We worship him for who he is not who we want him to be. Yahweh will not be manipulated. You can't use him to accommodate your agenda.

You could argue that every problem we face in the world could be reduced to some form of idolatry because every problem in our world stems from worshiping the wrong things.

This is why idolatry is such a big deal in the Bible. When we worship the wrong things, we become oriented in the wrong direction. We exchange who we were meant to be for a false identity. And when we do this, God has to wrestle it out of us.

Abuse. Racism. Greed. Violence. The list goes on, and each and every item in that list elevates something false, which ultimately misguides humanity.

Idolatry is the source of our problems. When we idolize something, we become fixated on what we think it can offer us. We resolve that it offers us something that will bring us fulfillment, but idols actually take something *away.*

They substitute the true, full, and eternal life God offers for something synthetic, superficial, and temporary. Idols limit your potential. They restrict your vision of who you were designed to be.

Here's what I mean.

An idol is crafted from our idea of perfection. We craft idols of the perfect spouse or the perfect job or the perfect body or the perfect _____. And once we form that idol, it commands our full attention. It becomes the image in front of our eyes and distracts us from reality. That's why it is so devastating when we learn the people we've idolized for their picture-perfect marriage end up in divorce or the people we've idolized for their job reveal they are burnt out or unhappy or the people we've idolized for their flawless body end up admitting they are still insecure or displeased with how they look.

We make these individuals—or the lifestyles they represent—into idols that promise happiness is found when we attain what they have to offer. And when—or if—you ever do, you realize that emptiness is still present inside of you, and you're left always wanting more.

Jesus once said, "No one can serve two masters. For you will hate one and love the other; you will be devoted to one and despise the other."[8]

Idolatry is taking some incomplete joy of this world and building your entire life on it.[9] It's making certain things—possibly even good things—*ultimate* things.

So what happens when an idol enters the Temple of Yahweh?

God's presence *leaves.*[10]

Don't forget, the Temple is a symbol. If you get tangled in the logistics, you'll end up struggling to solve this problem like an equation. God's presence is a mystery. It's universally present, yet circumstantially absent. For now, the message is this …

The worship of God is incompatible with the worship of idols. **When you fill the Temple with an idol, you empty it of God's presence.**

And when your Temple is full of idols and empty of God, eventually, you'll find yourself exiled in Babylon.

Go Tell The Exiles

In the time of exile, when the Jews were scattered, and Israel was occupied by foreign rulers, a prophet named Ezekiel had a vision.

Even though he is living in Babylon, in this vision, he is taken to the Temple of Israel to see what it has become.

When he arrives, God shows Ezekiel the cause of his people's exile …

The Temple is flooded with idols.

And every idol standing is a glaring reminder that the people's allegiance to Yahweh has been compromised.

When Ezekiel sees this, God asks him, "Have you seen what the leaders of Israel are doing with their idols in *dark rooms*?"[11]

This is important language because it reveals something about the nature of their worship …

They are *hiding.*

If what you do is done in the dark, it's because you're trying to conceal it. You're trying to cover it up. And what reason do we hide and conceal?

Shame. Insecurity. Fear.

(Hmm … where have we heard this story before?)

If the location of the vision wasn't explicitly identified, you might even mistake it for a garden where a man and a woman are rummaging in the bushes trying to cover up their nakedness.

But it's no use. The coverings are simply an illusion. God sees everything.

And as a consequence of the people's misplaced allegiance, God's presence is carried off to the east. He is no longer in the Temple.

It's a disheartening vision that clearly indicates a point of failure.

I'd bet there have been moments when this has been your picture of God. He's suddenly soaring up into the sky somewhere far away from us because of our sins and failures. Maybe it's more than moments. Perhaps this has become your *defining* image of God.

None of us were around when this vision was first delivered to the original audience, but I'm sure it was a tough crowd. Talk about putting salt in the wound. Ezekiel is tasked with informing his displaced community that the situation they find themselves in is all their fault.

Harsh … but necessary.

Because there is something important we need to recognize …

Truth is confrontational by nature. The message of Ezekiel is that people have traded the truth of God for a lie, and it has led them to a place of despair.

It's not because God wants to tear them down. It's because he wants to build them up. If those just sound like nice words that you're struggling to believe, then get this …

God doesn't leave the Temple to *abandon* his people …

He leaves to *gather* them.[12]

That's why Ezekiel's vision doesn't end with a picture of an empty Temple but hope for a new one.

A new Temple that is vacant of idols, full of people with new hearts and a new spirit. A Temple where they draw near to God as he draws near to them. Where they are responsive to the movement of his Spirit and awakened to his presence. A Temple where they honor truth and obey its decrees.[13]

A Temple full of beauty and prosperity. A Temple full of a rich and satisfying life.

God gives Ezekiel a vision in a place of desolation, and he's calling out to them from the future. He will restore their hope. He will restore their hearts.

"Afterward, the Spirit of God carried me back again to Babylonia, to the people in exile there. And so ended the vision of my visit to Jerusalem. **And I told the exiles everything the LORD had shown me.**"[14]

For Ezekiel, this vision comes with an assignment. He is given the responsibility of telling the exiles what he has seen.

And that isn't the only time this message has been delivered, because this isn't the only time it's happened. This is the role of all the prophets. They confront the lies and injustice and evils of people—not to condemn them but to save them.

It's the common thread in all of Scripture. It's the collective unified echo of the leaders of God's people. It's reverberating through the assembled pages of the prophets, poets, priests, and preachers that have encountered the God of the universe, and each time they have been given an assignment …

Tell the people.

This vision has a purpose: to comfort and inspire those that have wandered far from God. He will give a new heart, restore hope, and bring them home.

But the comfort of hope can only have meaning if it is grounded in reality.

You can't tell the lost, the poor, the oppressed, or the marginalized that things will get better if you are using those words as a sentiment. This vision isn't about changing perspectives or adopting a new attitude in a dire situation. It's a picture of a tangible reality in the days to come.

God *will* return. God *will* restore.

If what you hope for isn't true, then your hope is a lie.

But the God of truth speaks only the words of truth.

He has gone out to gather the people in exile from Babylon. He will give them a new heart and a new spirit. He will return to the Temple, and he will live among his people.

A Really Awkward Moment

A few years ago I was talking with a buddy of mine and his wife when he delivered some big news. He had just been offered a high-level position at a company out of state. He lit up with excitement as he explained all the events that led to the opportunity and how it aligned with some of his long term professional goals. Once he was done speaking I noticed his wife was quiet and expressionless.

I asked what she thought about the change ahead, but before she spoke a word I could already read the reluctance on her face.

She explained that even though she completely agreed the decision to move was best, she was still anxious about so much change and felt the decision would require some considerable sacrifice on her part. She was proud and happy for her husband but was mourning the reality of her own unmet hopes and dreams.

So there I was, staring at two different expressions for the same circumstance. It was awkward.

If the suspense of an entire community exiled in Babylon is becoming too much to bear then here is some relieving news—they eventually get to return home to Jerusalem. The story is outlined in Ezra and Nehemiah.

The exiles eventually rebuild the altar, lay the foundation of the Temple, and get together to celebrate their homecoming.

> But many of the older priests, Levites, and other leaders who had seen the first Temple **wept aloud** when they saw the new Temple's foundation. The others, however, were **shouting for joy**. The joyful shouting and weeping mingled together in a loud noise that could be heard far in the distance.[15]

I cringe just thinking about being there. Awkward is an understatement.

For years in exile, the people planned their return to Jerusalem. Their evenings were filled with lively discussions of the life that awaited them. They imagined what it would feel like walking the streets of their old home again. They formed big expectations that fueled their vision for the future.

And when the time came, some celebrated, and some grieved. Neither side was right or wrong. Sometimes there are simply different, yet appropriate, reactions to a particular circumstance.

Regardless of which people celebrated and which people mourned, one thing is evident in this story …

This isn't the Temple *either* group was hoping for—and here's why …

God's presence doesn't return.

When the prophet Ezekiel had his vision long before this greatly anticipated return to Jerusalem, there was a crucial piece in his message to the exiles …

> **I will give them singleness of heart and put a new spirit within them.** *I will take away their stony, stubborn heart and give them a tender, responsive heart so that they will obey my decrees and regulations.* **Then they will truly be my people, and I will be their God.**[16]

A better life isn't found by simply moving to a new location. You won't find fulfillment in external circumstances if you don't experience internal transformation. The people haven't changed—they brought all their problems with them. This clearly isn't the moment they've all been waiting for.

The exiles devoted themselves to stacking stones and laying the foundations for the Temple but neglected to address the problem of their hearts. They were one step closer on their journey, but miles from their destination.

And this is true of more than this ancient community. Many of us spend time crafting expectations of what a relationship with God should be like. We think, "If only God did this." Or maybe, "God should have done that, then all would have been made right." But when we deflect our problems, we never take the time to address the real issues within ourselves.

Many of us are spending a lot of time constructing a Temple for God to live in without ever building a door for him to enter. The heart is the way God will enter his new Temple—but ours have become like stone.

Sometimes we want—and even expect—this incredible life with God, trying to get back home, but never allowing him to change our hearts.

So if God is going to reenter the Temple, then we need a new heart— we need a new spirit.

God Came Home, and He Wasn't Happy

My wife and I have moved homes a few times. We love change, and so every couple of years, we are looking to shake things up and put our house on the market.

If you've ever bought and sold a house, there is a person you simultaneously love … and hate …

The inspector.

This person's job is to perform an inspection of the home and provide an exhaustive report of his or her findings. And let me tell you, a good inspector will find *everything*.

When we were preparing to sell our house, my wife and I worked hard to get it ready for the market. We patched up holes, painted over scuffs, and scrubbed floors and countertops. The place was spotless. Or so we thought—until we got a copy of the inspection.

Pages upon pages of issues. Thankfully it was nothing too costly, but the report included everything imaginable. From a thin crack on the outer outlet cover to the chip on the baseboard behind the couch, every detail was accounted for.

When you're trying to sell your house, you have nothing but animosity for this person. They shine a light on all the issues and hand you a bunch of chores and expensive projects. But when you're a buyer, you have nothing but gratitude. This person keeps you from signing a contract on a house with significant issues or in need of dire repair.

An inspector's job is to identify the issues and damages in the house. He does this to illuminate possibly unseen troubled areas that need repair so that the house can be restored.

Like I said—this person is easy to love … and hate.

Over time, the exiles of Babylon reestablished themselves in Jerusalem, but power changed hands from the Persian Empire to the Roman Empire. The same question was still on everyone's mind: when will God's messiah come? When will we be free from oppressive rulers and live in the freedom God has promised? When will God's presence return to the Temple?

When Jesus enters Jerusalem, many declare that the time has come. They praise his triumphant entry calling him the "Son of David."[17]

It's a subtle nod to the audience that God's presence has returned to the Temple. Just like the fire and pillar of smoke, **Jesus is the physical manifestation of God's presence.**

And upon his arrival, he first visits the house of God to make an inspection, and the report isn't good.

Apparently, this house, built to hold God's presence and bring hope to all nations, has been exploited for profit, power, and position. The leaders that occupy the Temple are seizing an opportunity to benefit themselves by taking advantage of the people.

So Jesus gets angry and starts flipping tables. I guess you could say some love him and some hate him.

"[Jesus] said to them, 'The Scriptures declare "My Temple will be called a house of prayer," but you have turned it into a den of thieves!'"[18]

Often this story is used to demonstrate that Jesus gets angry, but what is sometimes missed is *why* Jesus gets angry …

This Temple is not serving its true purpose—to be a place that directs the people toward proper worship.

And if the Temple is not serving its true purpose, how can God dwell among his people? And if God can't dwell among his people, then how will they live the lives they were meant to live? And if God's people can't live the lives they were meant to live, then how will they point the nations to right relationship with God?

A lot is riding on this Temple. But it's not about renewing the structure of a building; it's about building a structure for renewal.

This Temple may not be full of statues, images, or carvings … but it's still full of *idols*. It's still a place of misappropriated worship and bad religion. That means it's a Temple like all the other temples. And if this Temple is like all the other temples, it will never fulfill its unique purpose.

So when Jesus completes his inspection, he determines there is too much damage to repair. He says he will destroy the temple and raise it three days later.[19]

Wait, how could he do that? I couldn't tear down a woodshed and rebuild it in three days, let alone an entire temple built over 46 years with the help of thousands of people.

Not only was this statement ridiculous—it was offensive. Many people devoted their lives to restoring God's holy Temple. They put in all their effort; their blood, sweat, and tears. They meticulously stacked brick over brick. There have been architects and craftsmen passing their trade down from generation to generation, specifically for perfecting this building. It was the center of the community and a symbol of their identity.

But Jesus claims it's doing more harm than good.

"Do you see all these buildings? I tell you the truth; they will be completely demolished. Not one stone will be left on top of another!"[20]

This is the kind of thing that will make people angry. This is the kind of thing that would get a person *killed*. And that's exactly what the religious leaders conspire to do.

Why?

Because this Temple was a source of security. It was their way of building up confidence in who they were. It made them feel protected. It made them feel important. It made them feel significant. That means there would only be one reason for them to become hostile and violent …

This Temple was covering some form of the people's insecurity.

That's why a home inspection is necessary. We can make things look presentable cosmetically yet have significant problems in the foundation.

When people feel threatened, they take extreme measures to avoid feeling exposed. It's easy to criticize the religious leaders, but it's important to consider that they thought what they were doing was right. They thought they were following God's instructions found in Scripture. But according to Jesus, there is something they were missing …

"You search the Scriptures because you think they give you eternal life. *But the Scriptures point to me!* Yet you refuse to come to me to receive this life."[21]

Don't miss the connection: in this ancient culture, if someone is "searching the Scriptures," where do they go to read them?

The Temple.

The religious leaders are crying out for God's presence to return to the Temple, but unknowingly reject it when it comes through Jesus. They are hiding from God in the very place they think they will find him.

We all live in this temple. One we construct to make ourselves feel better. We use it to cover up our mistakes and failures. We use it to portray the image of ourselves we want others to see. We use it to hide from the things that expose who we truly are. We fill it with idols and chase the wrong things to find full life.

The Temple is a covering. It covers the people from feeling …

Naked.[22]

So what happens when the religious leaders are confronted with the idea of their coverings being removed? The same thing that happens in the Garden when Adam and Eve are confronted about their insecurities: they point the finger and try to cast blame.

The leaders rally the people around a common cause—that Jesus is to blame. Everything is his fault. He needs to be put to death.

I know it doesn't seem "nice" to threaten to destroy the Temple, but execution is an extreme course of action—especially when you read this …

"But when Jesus said 'this temple,' he meant his own body."[23]

What? That's kind of a HUGE detail Jesus left out. Couldn't he have avoided death with a little clarification? Was he killed because of a small misunderstanding?

The simple answer is yes. Jesus didn't have to die—he chose to die.[24] And it's for this reason …

The Temple became a covering of fig leaves, not much unlike the ones fashioned by Adam and Eve to conceal their shame. And this covering was insufficient. So God made the sacrifice to *clothe them.*

But we don't need to be covered in animal skins. We need to be clothed in a new kind of temple. When Jesus says he will raise the temple, he isn't talking about a pile of stones. He's talking about a body—his body.

And when Jesus is talking about his body, he's talking about more than his own flesh and blood.

He's talking about raising up … *a people.*

Connecting the Dots

My son has a collection of coloring books I like to break out as a distraction when his brain switches to Godzilla mode, and he gets the urge to destroy our house.

In addition to pictures, many of these books contain activities and puzzles. These were always throw away pages when I was young. I was never actually interested in completing a word search, drawing the other half of the picture, or tracing the line out of the maze. But there is one activity I did enjoy …

Connect the dots.

The task is simply to create the outline of an image and complete the picture. But honestly, you usually don't have to connect the dots to see what the picture is.

Even without the lines drawn in to define the image clearly, you can still likely guess what it is. Truthfully, it's not hard to recognize a zebra or a giraffe even in the absence of an outline. It's not a clearly defined image, but you get the gist.

It's no big deal when you skip a page from a coloring book, but that's also how some of us view our spiritual journey.

We're excitedly flipping through pages of our life, trying to select an image that excites us and quickly skipping over the ones that aren't already drawn in. Who wants to complete an assignment when you're opening a fresh box of crayons with your good pal ROY G. BIV[25] and ready to flood the pages with color?

Besides, even if you don't take the time to complete the picture, you get the gist—right?

But in order to recognize the value of this crucial stage in our spiritual journey, we need to take a seven-mile walk …

After the death of Jesus, all of his followers were devastated. There were reports of his empty tomb, and people were trying to make sense of it all. Two of them were leaving Jerusalem and headed to Emmaus—about seven miles away—and were talking about everything that had happened.

As they talked, the resurrected Jesus joined them, but the Bible says, "God kept them from recognizing him."[26]

Kind of an anticlimactic way to make your big reveal, don't you think? Isn't that the whole point of the resurrection? He could have stopped them in their tracks and delivered the ultimate, "I told you so."

But remember, this isn't about Jesus being *right.* The truth is secure in the truth. There is something else going on here that we need to pay attention to. As they are all walking, Jesus asks the two about the things that had happened in the previous few days. And he doesn't ask to acquire information. He's well aware of what took place because it all happened to him.

When Jesus asks a question, it's for our benefit, not his. He's inviting us to dig deep within ourselves to investigate what is happening in our hearts and minds.

And so they inform this person (they didn't realize was Jesus) about the story of Jesus. They said he was a prophet. He was a teacher. The religious leaders handed him over to be crucified. Now he's gone—the end.

But not really. There's a lot of gaps in their perspective. The Bible says this …

"Then Jesus took them through the writings of Moses and all the prophets, **explaining from all the Scriptures the things concerning himself.**"[27]

These two followers of Jesus had gotten so excited coloring all the pages that appealed to them they skipped the activity where they had to connect the dots. They figured they could make out a picture of what God was doing, but they didn't actually spend time forming a clear picture.

And if it happened to them, it can happen to us.

Jesus may be hidden from you, not because he isn't present, but because you haven't taken the time to connect the dots.

You might have tried to engage a relationship with God for the excitement of flooding your pages with color but skipped the necessary task of forming a clear picture.

And the task ahead is more than aimlessly moving a pencil from circle to circle. That doesn't work in coloring books, and it certainly doesn't work in faith. You have to connect the dots **in sequence.**

If you quickly carve a line between dot #1 and #50 and link every dot in a random pattern, you're going to create a tangled mess of zigzags that don't end up looking like anything.

Jesus helps these followers connect the dots of the Scriptures they knew—in the proper order—so that he could reveal the truth they hadn't yet recognized; which is this …

All of it was leading to him. He is the fulfillment and full picture of everything they had been waiting for.

Our world is full of more people that know *about* Jesus than actually *know* Jesus. What separates these two groups?

Connecting the dots.

And this is the hard reality of connecting dots …

You're going to have to draw definitive lines.

You can't form a picture if you refuse to mark the page. There isn't room for "maybe" in the Christian faith. Don't get me wrong; it's good to spend time searching. It's good to wrestle with your doubts. It's good to investigate various perspectives. It's good to challenge beliefs that don't quite make sense to you.

But we all know you can spend a lifetime trying to accumulate information while never actually making a decision.

And deciding to follow Jesus doesn't mean you have all the answers. That's why we have faith. It stands in the gap of what we don't know. It stands in the gap of what *no one* knows.

Please don't misinterpret what I'm saying. If you're unsure about God and you're trying to piece things together, you are absolutely doing the right thing. Maybe you're even reading this now because you're investigating a relationship with God. Don't take this as a criticism that you haven't made a decision yet. To you, I say, "Well done, keep going, and be ruthless in your search."

But here is the point I am making …

You will have to draw definitive lines to connect the dots at some point in your life. And if you connect the dots between the stories of Scripture, Jesus says what you're doing is completing a picture of him.

After some time, when these two disciples and Jesus finish their seven-mile walk, they have an epiphany: "… their eyes were opened, and they recognized him."[28]

And how do they recall what they felt at that moment?

"Our hearts were burning within us."[29]

I hope you've been paying attention. There is a significant contrast taking place here. In the garden, when Adam and Eve form a picture of a kingdom of their own making, their eyes are opened, and they feel guilt and shame. But on the road to Emmaus, when these two travelers form a picture of the kingdom of Jesus, their eyes are opened, and their hearts are set on fire.

This is the kind of life Jesus wants to give you. Not one cloaked in shame and insecurity, but one where you see him clearly—and your heart is on fire.

And that's true of more than just stories or prophecies in the Bible. As important as it is to connect the dots of the biblical narrative to give us a clear picture of Jesus, we also have to do the hard work of connecting the dots *in our own life.*

These ideas are useless if they remain words on a page written thousands of years ago. It's only valuable if it's lived—if it's experienced.

Theories can't stay theories. They need to be examined. Challenged. Proven.

The theory of Jesus is waiting to be tested in your life.

When God Breathes

You never chose to be born. Your existence was chosen for you.

That's true for all humanity—regardless of what you believe or your worldview. No matter how much we evolve, learn, or accomplish, from now until the end of the world, we will still have to humbly acknowledge that we played no part in our own creation. You did not make yourself. Your place was determined by forces outside of your consent or your control.

Whether it was luck or love—your life was a gift that you didn't give yourself.

But the Bible makes a case for the latter and describes the event like this …

"Then the LORD God formed man from the dust of the ground. **He breathed the breath of life** into the man's nostrils, and the man became a living person."[30]

At a biological level, humans are made up of atoms and molecules. These are the same elements that make up everything in the universe. What's interesting about this passage is that it claims God *formed* humans. It's like a potter molding clay into his desired image. God took the raw material of the universe and ordered it. Assembled it. Structured it. Shaped it. Assigned it. Moved it.

The Bible tells us in Genesis that God spoke everything into being. But when we zero in on humans, there seems to have been a different method. God took his time. He didn't simply speak them into existence—he *formed them* into his image. We are the craftsmanship of his artistic expression.

But what distinguishes humans from the rest of the created order is something else. We are more than dust. We have …

The breath of life.

That means when God breathes something comes to life.

This breath makes humans more than their natural instincts. It separates them from the plants and the animals. It equips them beyond the elements needed for survival. This breath of God gives them awareness, logic, and reason. It makes them conscious of their own existence.

Humans are more than raw material—they have consciousness. Adam awakens to the reality of his existence when God breathes into his nostrils.

And equipped with consciousness, we are not only aware of our existence—we are aware of our death. We know what it means to lose the life we have been given. We know what it means to lose the breath of life.

Even Jesus knew his time on earth would end. He was aware of his life, and he was aware of his death.

On the cross, his time had come ...

"Then Jesus uttered another loud cry **and breathed his last ....**"

But something unique happened when Jesus died. After he exhaled his final breath, it says, "And the curtain in the sanctuary of the Temple was torn in two, from top to bottom."[31]

Remember, the Temple was a *symbol* of God's presence. When Jesus dies, and the curtain is torn, it is a clear indicator that God is not contained inside the Tabernacle. Something happened in the death of Jesus that decentralized the presence of God.

But it wasn't just his death that was significant. It was his resurrection. When word began to spread from the women that discovered his empty tomb,[32] people were beginning to feel hope again. Their time grieving was spent thinking Jesus was less than they thought, but a resurrection would prove he was actually more. They hoped he could conquer the government, but this showed he could go even further and conquer the grave.

And there is more going on here than initially meets the eye.

Before the exile, when God's presence leaves, the people search for him inside the Temple, but he isn't there. When Jesus is resurrected, his followers search for him in a tomb, but he isn't there. It seems like the places people go to look for God leave them empty-handed.

The Bible asks, "Why do you search for the living among the dead?"[33]

They search in the tomb because that's where you leave those that have departed. The people that no longer have the breath of life.

The truth is, sometimes we look for life in a tomb. But it isn't there. Life is found where God breathes because when God breathes—something comes to life.

That's why Jesus appears to his disciples after his resurrection and says this …

"'Peace be with you. As the Father has sent me, so I am sending you.' **Then he breathed on them** and said, 'Receive the Holy Spirit.'"[34]

God breathes into Adam, and he becomes a living being. Jesus breathes on his disciples, and they receive the Spirit.

Maybe you've heard about this idea of "receiving the Holy Spirit," and it sounded like religious gibberish—literally.[35]

But here's what's most important about this idea …

God's presence is inhabiting the new temple.

The Holy Spirit finds a home among the followers of Jesus—to dwell with his people. This is made known in the New Testament.

"You are living stones that God is building into his spiritual temple."[36]

This is a paradigm shift. And as big as that is, it gets even more significant. Before, God dwelled in the Temple to live among the descendants of Abraham. But the idea wasn't to be exclusive. The promise God made was to bless the nations so *all people* could be made right with God. Because of Jesus and the indwelling of the Holy Spirit, that time has now come.[37]

> *So now you Gentiles are no longer strangers and foreigners. You are citizens, along with all of God's holy people. You are members of God's family. Together, **we are his house,** built on the foundation of the apostles and the prophets. And the cornerstone is Christ Jesus himself. We are carefully joined together in him, becoming a holy temple for the Lord. Through him, you Gentiles are also being made part of this dwelling where God lives by his Spirit.*[38]

The followers of Jesus form the new temple of God where he lives among his people.

And when we become the new temple of God's Spirit, we no longer have room for worthless idols or time for chasing worthless things. We have a full life and true purpose.

> *And what union can there be between God's temple and idols? For we are the temple of the living God. As God said:*

> *"I will live in them*
> *and walk among them.*
> *I will be their God,*
> *and they will be my people."*[39]

And don't miss what Jesus says *before* his disciples received the Spirit …

I am sending you.

Being the temple of God's presence comes with an assignment. We are instructed to go somewhere. To do something.

This is what we refer to as … a calling.

Something Is Calling You

At one point, you had an idea.

I'm not saying you've had ideas in general. All of us have all kinds of ideas all the time. No. I'm saying there is a specific idea you've had at one point or another in your life.

This idea didn't necessarily come from you. It was probably delivered by an outside circumstance—something you witnessed, experienced, or encountered.

I know you've had this idea because *everyone* has had this idea. It's been planted in all of our minds no matter who we are, where we come from, or what we've been through. With enough life experience, this idea presents itself to all of us.

If it's unclear, allow me to reacquaint you with this idea you had long before this moment. It should look, or sound, familiar—you've seen it in your own handwriting, spoke it from your own mouth, or heard it within your own heart. The idea is this …

I have unmet potential.

If that doesn't sound quite right, this idea may have adopted another phrase …

I'm capable of more.
There's something I have to do.
Just give me a chance.
I'll work harder.
Let me prove myself.
I need to do better.
I need to be better.
I can improve.
One day I'll show them.

No matter how you'd word it, they are all centered around the same idea, saying the same thing: there is something you have to offer that has yet to be revealed.

That's true for everyone, but there is a deeper layer when you apply the lens of Scripture. It's not just about becoming everything you *can* be. It's becoming everything you were *meant* to be. Everything you were designed to be. Everything you were intended to be.

Because your life isn't an accident. You were put here for a reason. You were made for a ...

Purpose.

And only when you're living your purpose are you able to reach your true potential.

That really isn't anything profound. Everything you used today was designed with a purpose. Your toaster. Your smartphone. Your car. Your computer. I mean, look around. Are you sitting on a chair or lying in bed? All of it specifically designed for the purpose it serves.

Even now, the only way you're even comprehending these sentences is because you're reading these words left to right, top to bottom.

Why?

Because that is how it was *designed*. Everything around you is assisting you to do whatever you're doing because it was created for a purpose. And if you assigned any of those things a different purpose, they wouldn't function to their full potential.

But you still have the freedom to assign it a new purpose. You can decide your couch is the best way to drive to work, but you'll end up frustrated with the results. That's because you're trying to make it do something it wasn't made to do.

If that's true of our everyday objects, what does it say about us?

You are a complicated, detailed, sophisticated, remarkable creation intentionally designed for a unique purpose.

That means you have been given a calling.

Maybe that idea seems scary to you. It can feel like your life has a narrow path with zero margins for error. But before you get anxious or worried you're doing the wrong thing and will need to completely uproot your life to become a missionary in Africa, just slow down for a moment. You've got some time. The earliest flight to Zambia isn't until tomorrow afternoon.

Now, I'm not going to sugarcoat this—there are some things God is calling you to do that you don't want to do. We've all had a Jonah moment when God is directing us toward Nineveh, and we are sprinting in the opposite direction. And why do we do this?

Because sometimes—if not most times—what God calls us to do feels uncomfortable.

But here's the thing we all need to come to terms with …

You will never ever reach your true potential if you hide in the bushes when God approaches.

Sometimes we protect our comfort at the expense of our calling. Our comfort zone is where we feel safe, where things are predictable, where we aren't put on the spot or put in a position to respond (or possibly lead), where things are familiar, where the future can be almost certain.

Your comfort zone serves as a nursing home for your calling and your true potential—a space they can quietly wait out the rest of their days undisturbed and rarely visited until their time is up.

Maybe you've heard someone say that you should consider stepping out of your comfort zone. When I hear that phrase, I get this picture of my neighborhood friends daring each other to ring the doorbell of the scary house we all thought was haunted on the corner of the street. Even if you get one of them to do it, they'll just take off running back to safety.

When you step out of your comfort zone, it isn't to collect a souvenir you can hold on to when you return. When you step out of your comfort zone, it's to *expand* your comfort zone. To make things that were once thought of as scary, as common.

Remember how you felt before the first day of high school? It was probably intimidating. You thought you wouldn't know your way around. You knew the classes would be harder. The homework would take more effort. But then as time passed, it really wasn't that scary anymore. It became familiar, and you realized you were capable.

Expanding our comfort zones is about growth, and growth is about working our way to our true potential.

Here's something we can all agree on …

If there is a God, and that God created you for a purpose, and if that purpose is known through a relationship with Jesus … then without a relationship with Jesus you will never know your purpose, and if you never know your purpose, then you will never reach your full potential.

For some of you, the jury is still out on the first, second, or third layer of that statement. But if you've gotten all the way to deciding Jesus is who he said he was, then you need to be aligning your life with his will if you want to live the life you were made to live.

And if you aren't, then you need to start now.[40]

Honestly, sometimes we are afraid of finding our calling. We assume when it's our turn to draw straws, we will inevitably grab the short one, meaning our assignment is something that will make us miserable for the rest of our days. If you've ever felt this way, trust me; I understand. In fact, there have been times, when weighing some of the options that have been placed in front of me, I automatically determined God was calling me to the one I wanted the least.

It feels like we were made to be martyrs.

But this perspective doesn't give God enough credit. He made you to enjoy the life he gave you.

Jesus asks his followers, "You parents—if your children ask for a loaf of bread, do you give them a stone instead? Or if they ask for a fish, do you give them a snake? Of course not!"[41]

God knows how to give good gifts.

Don't get me wrong—sometimes he *is* calling you to the thing you want least. But that isn't to torment you. We can be so stubborn and narrow-minded that we don't realize the path he has put before us leads to a place where we will thrive.

I love mashed potatoes, but for some reason, my son hates them. Last week he wouldn't try a bite of something I was trying to give him because he said it "looked like mashed potatoes."

It was ice cream!

But no matter how much I tried to convince him I wasn't trying to poison him, he wouldn't give in. I think a lot of times, the same thing happens with God. He's trying to offer us something he knows we will enjoy, but we are skeptical because of its appearance.

But looks can be deceiving.

That's why when you go to a restaurant, you aren't content to simply read the ingredients on the menu or look at the pictures on the wall; you came to eat.

Here's a verse worth memorizing … "Taste and see that the Lord is good."[42]

You can't live your calling through consideration and intention. You have to chew it up and swallow it. And Jesus says you'll be glad you did.

Because when you're living to your full potential, life is better than you could have imagined.

We are nearing the end, but there is one significant connection you need to make …

One of the biggest obstacles to living out your calling is your insecurity. When God is nudging you to take the stage of your life's purpose, it feels like the lights will expose all the parts of you that you try to cover up. This isn't just sappy stuff for emotional people.

Everyone has insecurities, and the people you think are immune have just become good at covering them up.

And this is a significant problem because **insecurity convinces you to settle for a cheap version of the purpose and calling God has for your life.**

Insecurity is the locked door shutting you out from your true potential. But when God breathes the Holy Spirit into us, it gives us the antidote to insecurity …

Inspiration.

And inspiration sets our hearts on fire. It gives us a clear vision of what we are here to do. It provides us with the confidence to reach out and grab the opportunities God has placed before us.

Inspiration is the antithesis of insecurity.

Insecurity is the feeling that we are incapable and inadequate. We step aside and allow others to pass ahead of us because we feel "less than" by comparison.

But inspiration fuels us with drive and purpose. It enables us to see something that needs to be created or accomplished and assures us we are the ones with the tools to make it happen.

Insecurity is hiding from God, naked behind the bush in the garden.

Inspiration is being inhabited by God, clothed as a new Temple.

Cultivate the Ground on Which You Stand

Sometimes we fall into this trap of watching the opportunities other people receive and wonder when we will get *our* shot.

We look at the fields that other people are farming and feel envy when their harvest comes, wondering when God will drop us on a plot of land just like it.

Ruth Haley Barton writes, "Narcissistic leaders are always looking longingly at someone else's field as somehow more worthy or more indicative of success. They are always pushing the limits of their situation rather than lovingly working the field they have been given."[43]

The ground on which you stand is the field you've been given to cultivate. That means the life you've been given is the life you've been assigned to develop. We look around at other people wanting the things or opportunities they have all the while missing out on what has been given to us.

Part of the reason we do this is because we place a higher value on the calling others have received. We elevate them as more important or significant in God's plan, and it makes us panic.

What is the root cause of this?

Scarcity.

Growing up with siblings, you learn how to keep an eye on the cake because every time someone grabs a piece, it's one more you won't be getting. It can be easy to feel anxious or desperate with a scarcity mindset. Whenever someone around you succeeds, it feels like there is less opportunity on the table for you.

Listen carefully and make a point to remember this—**God isn't going to run out of blessing.**

He's got more than enough to go around multiplied by infinity. But it does take time. The greatest blessing comes from developing a relationship with Jesus, and that takes a lifetime to cultivate. Sometimes it feels impossible to be patient. There are things we have our hearts set on, and we want them all now. We live in a culture of instant gratification, and it has conditioned us to expect immediate results.

But that idea doesn't come from God. In fact, he is reorienting us to look out far ahead.

To show you what I mean, let's take a look at the book of Zechariah. After so many years of suffering in Babylon, the Israelites were wondering if the time had finally come for their banishment to end and return home. The prophet Zechariah provides a message from God that essentially answers their question with a few more …

Are you ready to walk with God once again? Are you willing to be who you were called to be? Have you learned from the consequences of your decisions?

These questions were rhetorical, given through a series of dreams and visions—through some strange imagery—of the day that God's plan would be realized, and he would once again dwell among his people.

There's tons of great stuff here, but one section in particular echoes what we've been talking about, and it's this …

At one point in the vision, Satan is making accusations of guilt toward one of God's priests (because I guess he just decided to step into heaven for a quick visit), and God rejects the accusations and responds by telling some angels to "take off his filthy clothes."

Can you take a guess where this is going?

Then God says to the priest, "See, I have taken away your sins, and now I am giving you these fine new clothes."[44]

Don't forget, this is a vision filled with symbolic imagery, but the imagery conveys a message. When our coverings are insufficient, and we are made to feel ashamed, **God clothes us.**

And then he says this …

"Do not despise these small beginnings."[45]

Something is happening, and it starts off small—maybe even small enough to miss it. But the seed of what God is doing in your life takes time to grow. And just like a seed, you don't see what's developing under the surface. The blessing and calling and purpose you want to grab hold of comes from years invested in tilling barren dirt.

And when you've been digging, you'll start to feel tempted to *despise* the work. You might want to quit and throw down your shovel. Toss your handful of seeds and settle for something else—something easier.

But something that has a small beginning is working toward an end. And we are told that end is …

A temple.

Zechariah is pointing his people to the day that the new Temple will be rebuilt, and the people will follow the one true king.[46]

And Jesus says for you that time has come.

You've been given this field. It's the life you live. No one else has been given this life.

Only you.

You've been given something no other person has ever been given. You are the sole owner and operator of your life. It is utterly and absolutely unique. No one has ever lived where you are, around the people you're around, in the time in which you live, with the perspective you have.

Ever.

What is supposed to come with this revelation is a feeling of …

Gratitude.

Your life is a gift you've been given. And if this life is a gift, then the only way to honor it is to love it. To see it. To feel it. To value it. To be satisfied with it.

We get distracted, trying to copy other people. We look to celebrities, or artists, or athletes, or business leaders, and strive to be just like them.

While they can serve as inspiration, they can't offer you a blueprint for *your* life. If you work to be like them, then your pursuit is robbing you, and you are denying the world of who you were made to be.

You weren't placed here on this earth to become someone else. You were put here because God made a good creation, and in his goodness, love, and wisdom decided that you were a necessary piece of that creation.

Don't strive to be like some person who catches your attention. Strive to be like Jesus. Because in doing so, you will then become your authentic self. You will then become you.

The world doesn't need another _____. It already has one. And a copy of what already exists destroys the creativity that your unique design and purpose embody.

The world needs you.

The true you.

And the only way to uncover the true you is to become a temple of God's Spirit—to be filled with God's presence.

Snooze Button

During the night, when I'm getting ready for bed, I start planning out the next day. I have a list of things that need to get done, and I begin strategizing a way to be productive.

I form a vision of how to make the most of tomorrow and feel the motivation rise. I picture myself feeling energized, enthusiastic, and ready to seize the day.

I'm going to jump out of bed, make coffee, spend some time reading, work out, shower, get dressed, and then as if all that was nothing to me, I'll actually start the day.

The plan is in place. It'll be an early start, so I set my alarm and crawl into bed.

I'm so excited for the next day to begin I have trouble falling asleep. But eventually, I do. And then it's interrupted by that alarm I set what feels like just 10 minutes ago.

Wait … 5:00 am? That can't be right. I feel like I only got 3 hours of sleep. I just need a little more time.

Snooze.

Alarm.

Just a bit more. Snooze.

Alarm.

Snooze.

Alarm.

Not the start to the day I had planned. How many well-intended mornings have been destroyed by the snooze button? Now there's no time for coffee, reading, or workout. In fact, I'll have to move at lightning speed just to start work on time.

What happened to all that motivation? What happened to that vision for the day? It gently dissolved into the warm sheets and pillow absorbing my tired body.

The snooze button is a curse. It's a decisive action to sleep now and procrastinate starting the day. It mocks our idealistic plans and sells us on a tempting alternative …

Sleep.

It feels so good to fall asleep. It's a place your mind and your body go to rest. To run from work or responsibility. A place you don't need motivation. Where you can let everything go—if only consciously.

It's easy to fall asleep. What's hard sometimes is staying awake. We all know the moments when our eyelids begin to weigh a hundred pounds, and our necks have to springboard our falling heads.

Sometimes it's just too hard to stay awake. The followers of Jesus experienced this on the night before he was arrested. As he was praying in the garden of Gethsemane, he asked his followers to stay awake and keep watch. But in a short matter of time, they had fallen asleep.

"Couldn't you watch with me even one hour? Keep watch and pray so that you will not give in to temptation. For the spirit is willing, but the body is weak!"[47]

Jesus challenges his disciples to push through their exhaustion and be attentive.

Is it a sin to sleep? Not at all. But you fall asleep in more ways than one.

Jesus challenges us all to keep watch, but sometimes we drift off to sleep.

The disciples weren't the only ones tired. Jesus was human. This is clear from the grief and dread he experienced while praying in the garden. He had the same human need for sleep as any of his followers. So what is the difference between him and his disciples? How was Jesus able to stay awake but they weren't?

Jesus knew the dangers ahead. He knew what was at stake. These concerns kept him alert. They kept him sharp. They kept him …

Awake.

You can't sleep when you're restless. As much as we try to avoid it, it's healthy to be a bit restless. Not in a debilitating way, of course. But in a way that recognizes and takes seriously the dangers of falling asleep.

Like when you're on the highway late at night and counting headlights turns into counting sheep. If you nod off at the wheel, it will have severe consequences.

That's what makes following Jesus so hard; you don't get a break. You don't get to rest your eyes.

> *Awake, O sleeper,*
> *rise up from the dead,*
> *and Christ will give you light.*[48]

This sleep isn't about being stuck in bed. This sleep is about being stuck in sin. This sleep is about your spiritual consciousness drifting off to a state void of the calling and purpose you have received.

You can't become who you were meant to be if you aren't alert and attentive to the time at hand. Too many people are living their lives asleep. It's time to get out of bed. Don't delay living the way God desires.

Don't hit the snooze. It's time to wake up now.

The Final Wedding

There are many days I have to fight the urge to reduce the Bible to a bunch of restrictive rules, ancient history accounts, or campfire stories. But there is one description of the Bible that captures its essence above anything else …

A love story.

More specifically, a love story about a God that will do everything he can—short of inhibiting your ability to offer your love freely in return—to rescue and renew you. And how does this story end?

With a wedding.

And this wedding is not just the end of the Bible—it's the end of this world. The Bible says that the greatest gift God has for you is a proposal. He has made a covenant, delivered his vows, and now he awaits your response before carrying you home to his kingdom.

> For the time has come for the wedding
>   feast of the Lamb,
>   and his bride has prepared herself.
> She has been given the finest of pure white
>   linen to wear."
>   For the fine linen represents the good
>   deeds of God's holy people.[49]

The bride of Christ is the Church—the collective apprentices of Jesus. The invitation is given to all. **He has come to us in our shame and clothed us in white.**

Being naked in God's holy temple is about abandoning our hiding places and standing before God, fully exposed for who we are. It's about having the courage to trust that this God is good—that his way is best. It's about believing that to him, you have always been naked, and yet you have always been loved.

Being naked in God's holy temple is about taking responsibility for your life. It's about facing the consequences of your actions and moving toward the hope of new life in Christ.

Being naked in God's holy temple is about discovering who God really is. It's the process of deconstructing the synthetic god we've created to make room for the God who is the creator. It's wrestling through the night to defeat your false self and demanding the blessing that has been yours all along.

Being naked in God's holy temple is about embracing the vulnerability of transformation through the lens of Truth. It's hard to admit our faults and our flaws, but it's a necessary step in being made into the holy image of Jesus, which is really about being restored to our true humanity.

Being naked in God's holy temple is about reaching your true potential by understanding and embracing the calling God has placed on your life. It's about allowing God to give you a new heart and a new spirit so he can dwell with you as your partner to build his kingdom. It's about channeling God's mission and purpose through the life he has gifted you.

This is *how* you were meant to be. This is *when* you were meant to be. This is *why* you were meant to be. This is *who* you were meant to be. This is *where* you were meant to be.

This is what it means to expose your deepest insecurities to reach your truest potential—so you can stand …

Naked In God's Holy Temple.

ENDNOTES

INTRODUCTION

1   See John 3:3

PART I — NAKED

1   Seriously. Do you remember that thing? What athletic function did this serve? Nevertheless, it was dope.
2   Just a random example, not taken from my own life.
3   See Genesis 1:28
4   At least for men. Science is still trying to determine what could possibly attract women to men. It's probably our dad jokes and video game endurance.
5   Take it easy; this is a J-O-K-E. Some of my best friends are homeschool alums, and they turned out much better than me. But if you're reading this, I know you weren't that offended because the people that will get the most triggered about making fun of homeschooling shut the book when they read the word "sex." Ha! Got 'em twice! Boom, roasted.
6   But in an overly sexualized culture, that doesn't stop people from trying.
7   See Genesis 2:25
8   1 Samuel 17:38-39
9   For the record, I sometimes think we place ourselves too much into this story and reduce it to an allegory for the challenges we face in our own lives. That kind of reading misses the point, which is that God owns the victory and moved in historical ways to advance Israel. This is not a story about you; it is about David, the future king of Israel. But on the flip side, any good story is

relatable, so it's also not-*not* about you. We can find balance in making a personal connection with God that made a historical impact by working in David's life.

10 See Matthew 7:14

11 Genesis 3:7

12 Genesis 3:11

13 Genesis 3:12. Not cool, man. This is one of the conditions of fallen men: an inability to take responsibility. More on that to come.

14 See Genesis 3:13

15 The best teaching I have ever heard on this comes from John Mark Comer in a series done at Bridgetown church called *Fighting the World, the Flesh, & the Devil.* Listen to all 11 teachings, but he makes his point in the first two.

16 Genesis 3:7 (emphasis added)

17 Genesis 3:1

18 See Genesis 3:15. Additionally, check out an excellent explanation for this passage in the BibleProject's video titled, "The Satan and Demons" on YouTube.

19 I sincerely don't write this for shock factor. But I think it's essential to address the reality of real hurts and points of shame we carry. Sure, I could censor, but does sugarcoating a turd make it that much easier to swallow?

20 See Genesis 3:10

21 Genesis 3:21

22 You could make the argument that this statement summarizes all of Scripture. It's overly simplified, so *I* wouldn't. But *you* could.

23 We know you're trying to be polite, but please stop doing this.

24 Luke 15:22

25 Psalm 93:1

26 Psalm 104:1-2

27 I don't think Jesus would be offended by this comment, so you shouldn't either.

28 See Hebrews 4:15

29 Matthew 4:3

30 See Romans 5:14

31 Matthew 4:10

32 Matthew 7:24-27

33 Isaiah 53:3

34 John 11:35

35 John 11:25-26 (emphasis added)
36 This has become an essential practice for me as a father. I write a letter of reflection as a birthday gift to my children every year. They will be receiving these letters when they transition into adulthood. Each letter summarizes the events that took place that year but speaks life and encouragement for what I see in them and who I see them becoming. Each letter by nature is essentially a prayer of gratitude that God has given me the gift of these children. If you are a parent, this practice will form you as much as it hopefully forms them. Start now.
37 These two letters are very different from one another each year. I'll leave it to them to decide if they share them or keep them from curious eyes.
38 This definition is found in the Bridgetown series, *Fighting the World, The Flesh, & The Devil.*
39 Matthew 6:22-23
40 Genesis 3:6 (ESV—Emphasis added)
41 Exodus 20:17
42 *The Silence of the Lambs.* Sorry to use this creepy reference. This movie is extremely dark, but this line is powerful and reminds us how susceptible we are to desire what is in front of us.
43 Matthew 6:23
44 See Matthew 20:20-24
45 John 18:17
46 John 18:18 (emphasis added)
47 See John 21:9
48 Jon Tyson makes some incredible points about this story in his book *The Burden Is Light* (16-28). Here he argues that Peter's issues are rooted in comparison, which robs us from the unique calling God has given each one of us. Jon would say I shouldn't compare our books, but the truth is that his book is much better. Go read that one instead of this one. It wouldn't be an exaggeration to say it changed my life—twice.
49 In case no one has ever told you, I will: You aren't better than any professional athlete in any sport unless you are a professional athlete. They don't suck. Their opponent is better than them. And they are better than you.
50 The impact of contempt is beautifully articulated in Dallas Willard's book *The Divine Conspiracy* (150-155).

51 Romans 5:8 (emphasis added)
52 Genesis 3:23 (emphasis added)

PART II — IN

1   This information isn't important to the story, but I wanted to impress you because I'm, well, insecure.
2   If this describes you, I want to recommend the book that changed my life: *Emotionally Healthy Spirituality* by Pete Scazzero.
3   BibleProject gives a great summary of exile. Check it out https://www.youtube.com/watch?v=xSua9_WhQFE
4   See Jeremiah 29:4-7
5   Jeremiah 29:11 (emphasis added)
6   This is an extremely difficult skill and always maintains a large element of risk. Even the experts lose big. Don't quit your day job.
7   This is a real example from personal experience. I folded before the flop. Absolutely heart breaking.
8   I've heard this from so many sources I don't even know who to cite. For this one, I'll say C.S. Lewis. It's a safe bet.
9   Matthew 25:14-15
10 Matthew 25:24-25
11 That chicken is too good to be made with legal substances.
12 And I was right. So much information wasted on me, never to be used in a practical way. You can argue all day for a "well rounded" education, but I'll advocate you start selecting your major in middle school.
13 Esther 4:14
14 Esther 4:14 (emphasis added)
15 Of all the quotes I could use from *Star Wars,* unfortunately I had to pull one from the worst movie of the entire saga. This is from *Star Wars: The Last Jedi,* an absolute abomination to *Star Wars* lore. But this line is good. Give credit where credit is due. Therefore, this movie gets one credit.
16 Romans 5:3-5 (ESV)
17 Romans 8:18 (ESV, emphasis added)
18 Mark 4:35
19 Mark 4:38
20 Go ahead, but you'll never find out who the killer is or where the treasure is buried.

21 This view is outlined very well by John Lennox in *Determined to Believe?*
22 See 1 Samuel 8:5
23 And yet we keep doing this. If this is a struggle for you I sincerely recommend deleting your social media apps from your phone if even for a short period of time. Test this theory and see if you feel happier when you aren't constantly comparing your life to everyone else.
24 See 1 Samuel 8:10-17
25 Unless you're an irresponsible bank that created the housing bubble of 2008. Anyone else wondering how some of those people got bonuses? This is precisely why we need to talk about responsibility because we all recognize the injustice of when people are rewarded for bad decisions.
26 1 Samuel 12:20
27 1 Samuel 12:25
28 Exodus 16:3
29 Mark 8:36
30 Luke 14:28
31 This message is rooted in Matthew 16:24.
32 DM her on Instagram @leahzielich

PART III — GOD'S

1   Genesis 11:3-4 NIV (emphasis mine)
2   Read Genesis 12:1
3   Genesis 12:2 (emphasis mine)
4   See Genesis 22:2
5   Genesis 22:12
6   I first encountered this idea in a teaching from Rob Bell called "The God's Aren't Angry."
7   Genesis 22:13
8   This is probably the most important question a person can ask on their journey to discover who God is. There is a simple answer offered in several places in Scripture. We will certainly answer this question but not quite yet.
9   Genesis 22:14
10 See Genesis 25:24-25
11 Genesis 28:16 (emphasis added)

12 Genesis 32:27-28 (emphasis added)
13 The phrase or idea of names being recorded in a "book of life" is found several places in the Bible, but the verse where Jesus himself makes the connection is found in Luke 10:20.
14 Genesis 32:29
15 You're saying it now, aren't you?
16 Exodus 33:13 (emphasis added)
17 Exodus 33:18
18 Exodus 33:21-23
19 This is my paraphrase. See Exodus 34:6-7. Additionally, I would highly recommend *God Has a Name* by John Mark Comer. The entire book is a comprehensive breakdown of this very passage and how necessary it is to form our view of God's character.
20 I've never seen this point articulated better than in *God Has a Name* by John Mark Comer, (p.155-187). You could honestly replace this whole section with that entire book. If you do, Jesus just might add a room to the mansion he's prepared for you in heaven.
21 See John 10:10
22 See John 10:11-13
23 Acts 10:2
24 Acts 10:34-36
25 John 6:35
26 For a great breakdown of these views read *Four Views on Hell* edited by Preston Sprinkle. These are all biblical arguments, so you can be the judge for yourself which you find most compelling.
27 Luke 23:35 (emphasis added)
28 Mark 10:42
29 Mark 10:43 (emphasis added)
30 See John 1
31 Isaiah 43:11 (emphasis added)

PART IV — HOLY

1 These numbers are obviously always changing, but if you want the most current statistic, you can search for it through Barna who produces annual reports titled "The State of the Bible" for a particular year. 2019 is available here: https://www. barna.com/?s=Bible.

2 Speaking of *The Alchemist,* you need to read it. It's a story about following your dreams and finding your purpose. In a way, that's what this book is about, but I likely won't sell 65 mil. copies.

3 You might have a version that says "Study Bible" or maybe a title that excludes the word "Bible" altogether. But the vast majority will say "Holy Bible."

4 But we can start the trend. Who's with me?

5 Genesis 2:3

6 See Exodus 3:5

7 See Exodus 12:16

8 Easter Egg—remember this point in Part II? Look, here it is again!

9 Exodus 15:11 (emphasis added)

10 Leviticus 11:45 (NIV)

11 This is a way, way, way too simple interpretation of this passage, and it's only one layer of what God is saying to his people. But it most certainly is a layer of what God is saying.

12 John 8:31-32 (emphasis added)

13 This argument is made beautifully in *Unbelievable?* By Justin Brierley (51-70).

14 If you're a believer, this is where you need to demonstrate some humility. Although the Bible makes it clear that God is the source of truth for all people, the next step is interpretation. All of us are at least a little wrong about something. That's why we have so many denominations within Christianity—each one thinking they have it right. Not to mention a lot of horrible things have been done in the name of Jesus because someone felt enlightened. Again, maintain your convictions with humility.

15 Romans 12:2 (emphasis added)

16 Luke 6:49

17 If that sounds harsh, just know I place myself in this category from the time I entered middle school to the time I graduated high school. Pathetic? Yep. Hence, why I am writing this book that I hope teaches people something I eventually learned—that there is something else actually meaningful and worthy of our admiration and imitation. If I've done a terrible job up to this point in communicating what that is, allow me to do so here … it's Jesus.

18 This phrase, or similar variations of this phrase, occur hundreds of times throughout scripture. But a specific example that captures this point would be Revelation 1:17-18—"When I saw him, I fell

at his feet as if I were dead. But he laid his right hand on me and said, "Don't be afraid! I am the First and the Last. I am the living one. I died, but look—I am alive forever and ever! And I hold the keys of death and the grave."

19 Romans 3:23
20 I really thought hard about making a connection to baptism with this metaphor, but that would be too cheesy … right? Unless you're reading this thinking it's a great connection. In that case, I thought of it first and take full credit.
21 Psalm 27:1 (emphasis added)
22 John 19:13 (emphasis added)
23 Strong's Greek 3,038 and 1,042, respectively.
24 There is an explanation for this in Star Wars lore, but I'll let you track it down on the internet. Perhaps you need to protect your virginity as well.
25 Luke 6:43-44 (emphasis mine). By the way, I have never seen a bramble bush. I just know they don't produce grapes.
26 I have never heard anyone actually say this.
27 Galatians 5:22-23
28 Metaphorically speaking. Trees can't swallow pills, either.
29 Ephesians 6:12
30 See Joshua 5:13
31 Joshua 6:4-5
32 Ephesians 5:8
33 Isaiah 6:7
34 I first read this in *The Divine Conspiracy* by Dallas Willard.
35 See Isaiah 6:9-13
36 Mark 1:15, NIV (emphasis added)
37 Strong 3,340
38 1 Peter 2:2-3
39 1 Corinthians 3:2-3 (emphasis added)
40 Romans 8:6
41 John 8:7
42 John 8:10-11 (emphasis added)

PART V — TEMPLE

1 Leviticus 26:1

2 But if you'd like to prove me wrong, I'd suggest Exodus 25:23. If anyone asks you about it, just tell them this verse changed your life.
3 Exodus 25:8-9 (emphasis added)
4 For an incredible book fully dedicated to this idea, check out *With* by Skye Jethani. It outlines the unhelpful ways we posture ourselves toward God and helps us work toward, as the title indicates, a life we should spend with God.
5 Exodus 40:38 (emphasis added)
6 1 Kings 8:27-29
7 Exodus 20:2-4
8 Matthew 6:24. This reference is specifically about money, but what stronger argument could be made for idolatry than money?
9 This idea is from *Counterfeit Gods* by Timothy Keller.
10 See Ezekiel 10
11 Ezekiel 8:12 (emphasis added)
12 This idea is clear throughout the book of Ezekiel, but it is also echoed in the parable of the lost sheep taught by Jesus. God leaves to search for his people.
13 See Ezekiel 11:18-21
14 Ezekiel 11:24-25 (emphasis added)
15 Ezra 3:12-13 (emphasis added)
16 Ezekiel 11:19-20 (emphasis added)
17 See Matthew 21:1-11
18 Matthew 21:13
19 See John 2:19. It is important to note this story occurs much earlier in John's account than in the other gospels. This is because it is either a separate occasion or the author intentionally restructured the timeline for a specific purpose.
20 Matthew 24:2
21 John 5:39-40 (emphasis added)
22 Bruxy Cavey makes a similar point and has a great section about how Jesus came to shut down religion in his book *Reunion.* This is one of the most clear presentations of the gospel I've ever read, and I couldn't recommend it highly enough.
23 John 2:21
24 See John 10:18
25 Red, orange, yellow, green, blue, indigo, violet in case you never learned the colors of the rainbow.

26 Luke 24:16
27 Luke 24:27 (emphasis added)
28 Luke 24:31
29 See Luke 24:32
30 Genesis 2:7
31 Mark 15:37-38 (emphasis added)
32 Side note: the *entire Christian movement* began with the testimony of these female disciples of Jesus. It seems God was more than comfortable assigning women important roles in Church leadership. Just saying.
33 Luke 24:5 (NIV)
34 John 20:21-22
35 Shoutout to our charismatic/Pentecostal friends. I've never spoken in tongues, but more power to you!
36 1 Peter 2:5
37 For some great perspective on God's people becoming the new Temple, read *Reappearing Church* by Mark Sayers, pp. 83-93. It should be required reading for all leaders of faith in Jesus.
38 Ephesians 2:19-22
39 2 Corinthians 6:16
40 I'm not just saying that. You should literally close this book and start praying.
41 Matthew 7:9-10
42 Psalm 34:8
43 This is from Ruth Haley Barton's book *Strengthening the Soul of Your Leadership: Seeking God in the Crucible of Ministry,* 111.
44 Zechariah 3:4
45 Zechariah 4:10
46 See Zechariah 6:12-13
47 Matthew 26:40-41
48 Ephesians 5:14
49 Revelation 19:7-8

THANK YOU

Leah, for letting me sneak out to write. For giving me honest feedback. For the phone call that supplied full affirmation that this book was meant to be written. For being my best friend and walking with me every step of this journey. For everything you've done for me.

Family, for the influence you have had on me. For the role you have played in my life. For your love and sacrifice. For your support and encouragement.

Bonnie, for the first hour we ever spoke. That conversation was a flood of validation. For helping me move forward to take the next steps.

Jeremy, for saying yes. For weighing every single word, dissecting every metaphor, and challenging every idea.

Various authors, for taking my call and providing encouragement, wisdom, and guidance to a rookie on the field.

Friends, for your support. This book began years ago through the conversations, arguments, investments, and emotions we've shared that have formed me into who I am now. If I could list you all by name it would be longer than the book itself.

Reader, for taking the time to consider the ideas presented in these pages. Whether you loved it or hated it, agreed or disagreed, you took time to read it. I am unspeakably grateful and honored that you did.

ABOUT THE AUTHOR

Matt studied Bible & Religion at Anderson University, and completed an MAT at Fuller Theological Seminary. After working in youth ministry for 10 years with middle and high school students, Matt began working at Grand Canyon University to work with young adults and fulfill a calling to become an author.

Matt lives in Phoenix, Arizona with his wife, Leah, and their two children, Kieren, and Kinsley.

If you'd like to contact Matt you can visit his website at www.mattzielich.com.

Made in the USA
Monee, IL
26 September 2021